The Final Whistle

David Orme lives in Winchester, where he has written a wide variety of poetry text books and picture books for young children. He spends a great deal of his time in schools performing and writing poetry, and encouraging children and teachers to take an active interest in poetry.

Ian Blackman was born in Hastings and supports Brighton and Hove Albion. An ex-PE teacher, he now lives in Norfolk and runs workshops, using sport as a natural inspiration to write. His ambition is to be writer-in-residence for a football club . . .

Marc Vyvyan-Jones lives in Bristol and supports Bristol City (the Robins).

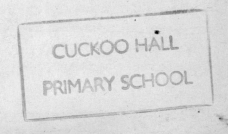

Also available from Macmillan

NOTHING TASTES QUITE LIKE A GERBIL
and other Vile Verses
chosen by David Orme

REVENGE OF THE MAN-EATING GERBILS
More Vile Verses
chosen by David Orme

UNZIP YOUR LIPS
100 Poems to Read Aloud
chosen by Paul Cookson

MY GANG
Poems about Friendship
chosen by Brian Moses

READ ME
A Poem for Every Day of the Year
chosen by Gaby Morgan

TONGUE TWISTERS AND TONSIL TWIZZLERS
More Tongue Twisters
chosen by Paul Cookson

THE FINAL WHISTLE

The Total Football Poem Experience

Football poems
chosen by David Orme

With football facts
by Ian Blackman

Illustrated by Marc Vyvyan-Jones

MACMILLAN
CHILDREN'S BOOKS

'Ere We Go! first published 1993 by Macmillan Children's Books
You'll Never Walk Alone first published 1995 by Macmillan Children's Books
We Was Robbed first published 1997 by Macmillan Children's Books
They Think It's All Over first published 1998 by Macmillan Children's Books
This edition published 2000 by Macmillan Children's Books
a division of Macmillan Publishers Limited
25 Eccleston Place London SW1W 9NF
Basingstoke and Oxford
www.macmillan.co.uk

Associated companies throughout the world

ISBN 0 330 48025 1

1 3 5 7 9 8 6 4 2

A CIP catalogue record for this book is available
from the British Library.

Printed and bound in Great Britain by
Mackays of Chatham PLC, Chatham, Kent

'ERE WE GO

Contents

Football Facts Ian Blackman

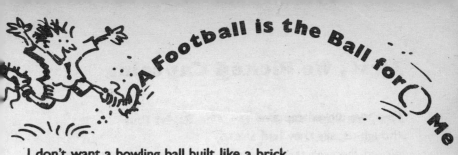

A Football is the Ball for Me

I don't want a bowling ball built like a brick
and volleyball is horri-ball, it gets on my wick.
I want a ball, a ball, a ball you can kick.

I wouldn't want to hit it with a wooden hockey stick
and to chuck it at a wicket in cricket is sick.
I want a ball, a ball, a ball you can kick.

My superball'll bounce off a wall dead quick
but a ball so small ain't at all worth a flick.
I want a ball, a ball, a ball you can kick.

Though netball's cool and baseball's slick,
there's only one ball game they just can't lick.
I want a ball, a ball, a ball you can kick.

One ball I need. One ball I'd pick.
I don't want six for a juggling trick.
I want a ball, a ball, a ball you can kick.

There's just one game with which I click.
Football, through thin and thick.
Football wins my voting tick.
Football, or my name's not Nick.

So I want a ball
a real ball
a proper ball
a ball you can kick.

Nick Toczek
Bradford

7

First, We Picked Captains

First, we picked captains,
though usually they had already
picked themselves.
Sometimes they just said it,
'I'll be captain,' and we pretended
our happy agreement.
It was easier that way,
and dusk was falling
so we needed to get started.

We stood in a line and the captains picked us.
'My first pick,' one would usually say,
and the other agreed, because that was easier,
and he never wanted
the boy that Billy picked anyway.

After they picked us, we lined up behind them,
always knowing who should be last.
But sometimes it happened
the usual last hadn't come to play,
had the bellyache, or was looking after
his little sister,
and someone else stood not wanting to be
the one not chosen, the one left over –
who never even got in the line with the captain
because already the rest were piling
their goalpost jackets and spreading for 'centre'.

Then, even the last-chosen would chase like mad
for a miracle goal, and their wild admiration –
though soon the ball was getting greasy
in the dew-sodden grass, and skidded away
off your boot in the wrong direction,
and the other side took it and easily scored,
and everyone shouted you'd kicked the wrong way.

John Loveday
Norwich

The Ball Talks in its Changing Room

I'm the star really. I'm the one
the crowds have come to watch.
I don't let it worry me. Before the match
they check me carefully, make sure
I'm really fit. After all
I have to take more pressure
than the rest of them. And then
it's the usual jokes about
there being more hot air in
the commentators than in me,
and the ref puts his arm around
my shoulders and says he hopes
I'll have a good game, no need
for a substitute, and off we go
to lead the players out. No time
for second thoughts once we start:
I'm in the middle of it all the way
with everybody shouting for me,
cheering as I dodge around the tackles,
or slide out of reach of players
who just want to put the boot in.
The crowd is all for me, willing me on,
praying that I'll reach the net,
and when I do, roaring with delight.
I take it as my due. The lads are all right
but, when all's said and done, Desmond,
they'd be nothing without me.

Dave Calder
Dundee United

I'm Jennifer Jones

(or, Antelope Jones . . .)

I'm Jennifer Jones and I make 'em all gasp
as I steal the ball neatly out of their grasp
pass to the centre and dodge to the side
skipping away from a tackling slide
collecting the cross that follows the throw
and shoot for the goal like a shaft from a bow.

I'm Jennifer Jones and I play on the wing;
I turn on a penny and I make the ball sing
as it curves and it spins past the gloves
on the hands of the keeper who LOVES
landing in mud and picking the ball
from the back of the net where I place 'em all!

Trevor Millum
Hamilton Academicals

J.J.

J.J. is O.K.

⑪

Playing for the School

Looking lively, running out,
yellow strip, boots all shiny with dew.

November morning. Air brisk on cheeks,
on knees. Puffing clouds. Then Sir

shrilling his whistle and black rooks
coughing in the sticks of trees.

Booted ball thudding, slithering
like a greased pig. Ninety minutes'

muscled battling. Mud all over.
Bruised warriors trudging in.

Tired. Winners. Hot as boiled eggs.

Matt Simpson
Liverpool

12

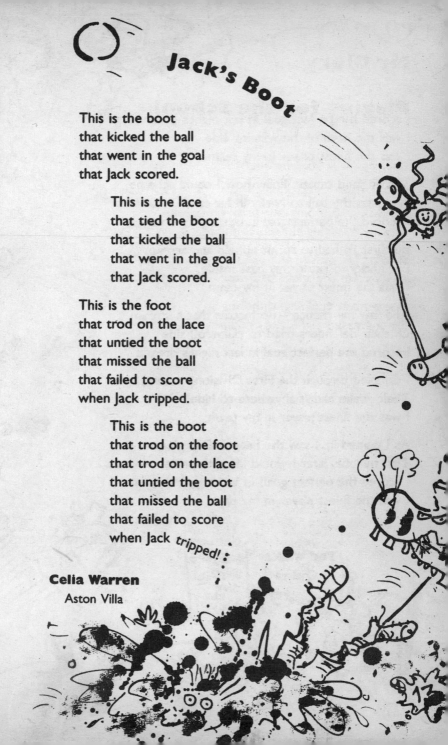

Jack's Boot

This is the boot
that kicked the ball
that went in the goal
that Jack scored.

This is the lace
that tied the boot
that kicked the ball
that went in the goal
that Jack scored.

This is the foot
that trod on the lace
that untied the boot
that missed the ball
that failed to score
when Jack tripped.

This is the boot
that trod on the foot
that trod on the lace
that untied the boot
that missed the ball
that failed to score
when Jack tripped!

Celia Warren
Aston Villa

My Glory

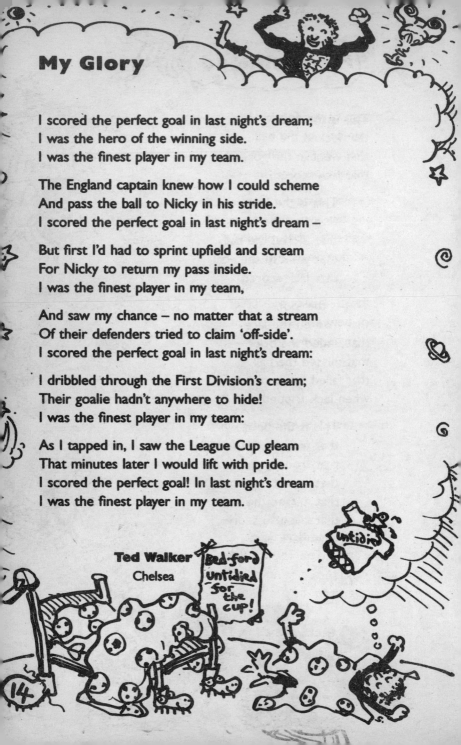

I scored the perfect goal in last night's dream;
I was the hero of the winning side.
I was the finest player in my team.

The England captain knew how I could scheme
And pass the ball to Nicky in his stride.
I scored the perfect goal in last night's dream –

But first I'd had to sprint upfield and scream
For Nicky to return my pass inside.
I was the finest player in my team,

And saw my chance – no matter that a stream
Of their defenders tried to claim 'off-side'.
I scored the perfect goal in last night's dream:

I dribbled through the First Division's cream;
Their goalie hadn't anywhere to hide!
I was the finest player in my team:

As I tapped in, I saw the League Cup gleam
That minutes later I would lift with pride.
I scored the perfect goal! In last night's dream
I was the finest player in my team.

Ted Walker
Chelsea

14

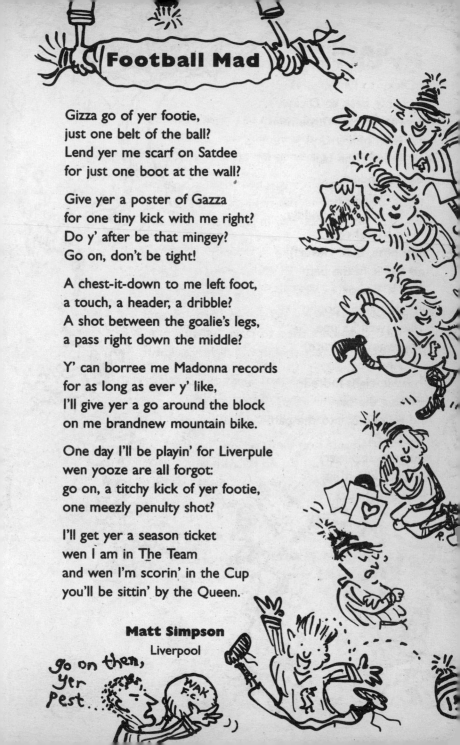

Football Mad

Gizza go of yer footie,
just one belt of the ball?
Lend yer me scarf on Satdee
for just one boot at the wall?

Give yer a poster of Gazza
for one tiny kick with me right?
Do y' after be that mingey?
Go on, don't be tight!

A chest-it-down to me left foot,
a touch, a header, a dribble?
A shot between the goalie's legs,
a pass right down the middle?

Y' can borree me Madonna records
for as long as ever y' like,
I'll give yer a go around the block
on me brandnew mountain bike.

One day I'll be playin' for Liverpule
wen yooze are all forgot:
go on, a titchy kick of yer footie,
one meezly penulty shot?

I'll get yer a season ticket
wen I am in The Team
and wen I'm scorin' in the Cup
you'll be sittin' by the Queen.

Matt Simpson
Liverpool

go on then,
yer
Pest...

Goal!

It's Dicky to Dirty,
And Dirty back to Dicky ...
He swerves past three men
    (Oh, he's tricky)
And he lofts the ball
Into the middle,
A pin-point pass,
    Which finds Diddle;
Diddle back-heels
(Very neat, that, clever!)
And lays it in the path
    Of Trevor,
Our six million pound
Striker (well 25 pee
If you want the truth)
    And he
Drives it, right-footed;
It strikes the bar
And rebounds into the path
    Of Pa
(Our oldest player)
But unluckily it hits
His walking stick ...

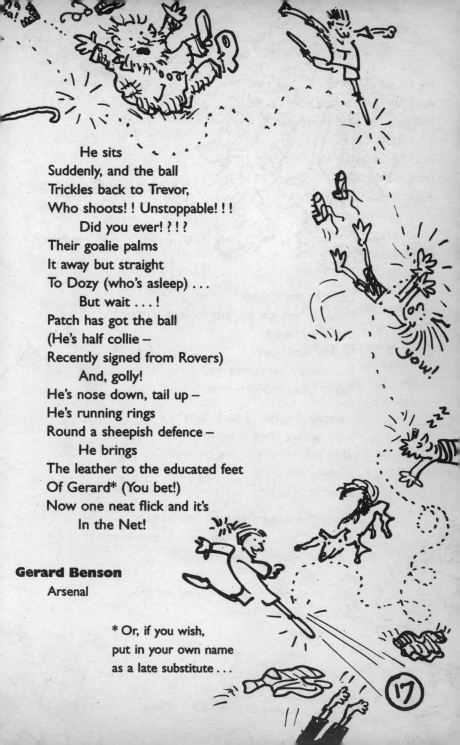

He sits
Suddenly, and the ball
Trickles back to Trevor,
Who shoots!! Unstoppable!!!
      Did you ever!?!?
Their goalie palms
It away but straight
To Dozy (who's asleep) ...
      But wait ...!
Patch has got the ball
(He's half collie –
Recently signed from Rovers)
      And, golly!
He's nose down, tail up –
He's running rings
Round a sheepish defence –
      He brings
The leather to the educated feet
Of Gerard* (You bet!)
Now one neat flick and it's
      In the Net!

Gerard Benson
   Arsenal

      * Or, if you wish,
      put in your own name
      as a late substitute ...

Little Beggars

Little beggers them!
Look at 'em, go on, just look at 'em –
slidin' and hackin'
hackin' and slidin'
like there's no tomorrow,
like it don't much matter.

Tuesday mornin', I was out there
right where they is now
with me roller and me prodder
all over the shop
all of it.

Then Thursday, I had me line painter
that ain't easy, I can tell yer
not like what it looks –
no Mister.
You soon see if you've rolled him flat
aye, that yer do.

Then this mornin', I was here at five
before all those horrible rough boys
was up, I'll be bound,
puttin' in them flags
and hangin' nets
and unlocking changin' rooms.

Not that you'd credit it
lookin' at it now
it's a proper disgrace
– shouldn't be allowed.

Ian Joyce
Leicester City

19

A Striker's Nightmare

Twelve games without a goal,
His leanest time in years.
His head begins to roll
Tormented by the jeers.

He cost a hefty fee
To spearhead the attack.
His scoring pedigree
Now stretches on the rack.

He scores the goals in training
And puts the crosses away.
His confidence is waning
'You've got to score today.'

Last week he scraped the bar,
And also hit a post.
He wears it like a scar
This run he dreads the most.

The winger tricks to shine
He beats one man then two,
He makes it to the line
And crosses deep for you;

A dummy run
Has found you space –
Now one v one
You soar with grace.

His worried head just met
The ball he arrowed down
The ball is in the net
The keeper wears the frown.

The home crowd chant his name.
Once more he is adored.
Relief replaces shame.
'At last you've . . . . . . scored!'

Ian Blackman
Brighton and Hove Albion

21

Bird's-Eye View

Come on City. Come on Rovers.
Up United. Up the Rangers.

Like football? Oh no.
Love football?
Over the moon about football? Oh yes, yes yes.
Couldn't care a chirp who wins,
                who loses.
Couldn't tot a tweet about the skills.
'Offside'
The referee who needs bi-focals.
'Our ball'
The fouls, free-kicks, defensive walls, the clever
corners or near misses.
'Gooaall!'

                peck peck peck
            hop   hop
        flap   flap

I just enjoy chaotic crowds
(when they've gone home),
    because 80,000 people equals
        800,000 titbits
(when they've gone home).

peck peck peck
    hop hop
      flap   flap

Terraces piled high with half-hot dogs in buttered buns,
samples of sandwich, scraps of sausage roll, crisps and
chips, and fruits of every flavour you could mention.
Eat until we're sick, sick, sicker than a parrot
(when they've gone home).

peck peck peck
    hop hop
      flap   flap

Couldn't care a chirp who loses,
couldn't tot a tweet who wins,
but I wouldn't mind a replay.

peck peck peck
    hop hop
      flap   flap

**Up United. Up the Rangers.
Come on City. Come on Rovers.**

Mike Johnson
Blackburn Rovers

23

Jambo

NO STUDS

Jambo playing football on the back field. His jeans rolled up to his knees covered in mud. Boots with no studs slipping and skidding. No-one watches except the tall cooling towers of the power station in the distance. No-one cheers him on.

CROWDS ON TERRACE

But as soon as Jambo scores, he's floating across the turf of Wembley Stadium. The stray dog yapping at his heels that jumps up to lick his face is the team captain's bristly embrace. And the women on the landings in the block of flats behind are the crowds on the terraces, waving banners that aren't really wet sheets after all. Even the hard-faced kids skiving off school round the back of the burnt-out garages look like they might want to line up for his autograph.

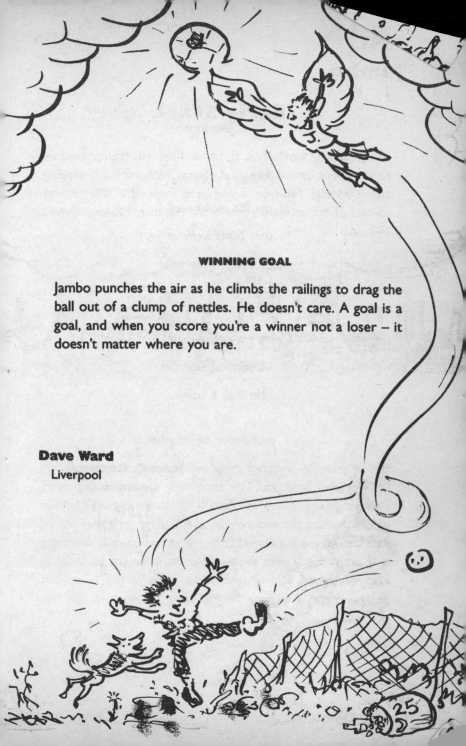

WINNING GOAL

Jambo punches the air as he climbs the railings to drag the ball out of a clump of nettles. He doesn't care. A goal is a goal, and when you score you're a winner not a loser – it doesn't matter where you are.

Dave Ward
Liverpool

Uuurrrh! Who's been sucking my book?

Early Start

Where does he

get his skill from;

that body swerve

and fancy footwork?

He's a natural, sir.

Dribbled since

he was a baby.

John C. Desmond
Leeds United

26

A Passing Movement, with Nicknames

'Ghost' goalie bowls it to 'Badger'
who spreads it to 'Headbutter' Case.
He punts it high to 'The Fat Man'
who nods it to 'Old Fungus Face'.
'Face' holds it, flicks it to 'Skinhead'
(who's bald as an OAP coot),
his laser-beamed pass reaches 'Chalky'
who slips it to 'Six-Gunner' Shoot.
'Six' looks up, toes it to 'Loony'
who, foot on the ball, picks his nose
then he shimmies
and shakes
and nutmegs his man
and lobs it across to 'Red' Rose.
'Red' is a tricky big turnip
and he touches it off to 'King' Cole
who in turn traps the ball
on the penalty spot
and crashes it
into
the

Wes Magee
Swindon Town

27

The Soccer Ghosts

There is a tale that must be told
About the soccer ghosts
That hang above the long white line
Between the upright posts.
  And in these goals they lurk by day
  Around the hour of three
  While in the evening's floodlit green
  They somehow get in free.
The striker thinks his header's in
But then he sees the ball begin
To spin outside the tall white post
Deflected by an agile ghost.
  The keeper's luck sometimes can shine
  The ball was booted off the line
  The keeper turned to thank his mate
  No-one there to congratulate!
This tale my friend I know is true
Just ask to hear the shooter's view
The many times that they have seen
A shot hit clean, that should have been
  A Goal
    I hear you say, 'But goals are scored
    There can't be soccer ghosts'
    I tell you sometimes ghosts get bored
    Haunting between the posts.

Ian Blackman
Brighton and Hove Albion

Off School

As the doctor asked him to,
he rinsed his throat with vinegar
then ate a bag of kumquats.
And soon the bugs had decomposed,
so he banged his bedroom door,
then hurried down the stairs.
Where was he escaping to?
Not school! Great Crikes, the thought!
He was heading for the park, of course,
with his scarf around his neck,
and underneath his jacket
a football. Would he play alone?
You bet! Unless you count the ducks
he curved those corners to,
or the sheep whose heads he found
when he floated freekicks in,
or the drunk he just persuaded
to sway around in goal.
And what more useful way to spend
a well-earned day off school?

Matthew Sweeney
West Ham

29

Own Goal?

We were due for a Cup Quarter Final
In the Junior League this weekend;
We'd trained hard, to make sure
That we'd get a large score –
But were dealt a grave blow by a friend.

Our captain, Ben Jones, is the reason
They've cancelled our Cupwinners' dream;
'Twas the worst of all shocks
When he caught chicken-pox
And then shared it all out with our team.

So we've penalty spots of our own now
And we certainly know what's the score,
For they won't let us play –
We're infectious they say –
And the upshot is we're feeling sore.

For a kick-off, we're out of the running –
They say we can't muster a team;
So, despite all our fuss,
They've disqualified us –
But, with luck, things aren't quite what they seem . . .

For (a week ago) Ben had a party . . .
He invited round all of his friends
Which included a few
Of the players he knew
From football teams other than Ben's.

And any day now, if we're lucky,
These players will show some fatigue
And start spreading their spots –
So what choice have they got
But to cancel the whole of the League!

Trevor Harvey
Arsenal

spotting'em Forest

"spot the ball" competition

31

'L' Plates on my Football Shirt

When I play football for the football team at school
no-one takes me seriously, they think I'm just a fool.
My right boot's on my left foot, my left is on my right,
my socks are on my arms and my shorts are far too tight.

I have shin pads on my chin just in case I'm fouled.
My shirt is full of holes, inside out and upside down.
The laces on my boots are nearly five miles long.
I need two weeks before each match so I can put them on.

They told me to play sweeper so I borrowed my mum's
        Hoover
and swept up their forward's shorts with a brilliant
        manoeuvre.
They asked about my shooting and how I could attack
so I got out my rifle but they made me put it back.

I told them that my dribbling was the best they'd get
then dribbled down their shirts and made them soaking wet.
They asked me to play winger, I said I couldn't fly.
'Well mark your man instead' so I gave him two black eyes.

'Free kick!' said the Ref, so I did and watched him fall.
Nobody had told me that I had to kick the ball.
In view of this the Referee gave the other team the kick.
I was told to build a wall but I couldn't find a brick.

In the end there's only two positions I can play:
left back right back in the changing rooms all day.
I'm only a beginner and someone could get hurt
so I don't have a number but an 'L' plate on my shirt.

Paul Cookson
Everton

32

Are You Sure We Are Up The Right End

United! United! United! United! United! United!

United! United! United! United! United! United!

United! United! United! United! United! United!

United! United! United! United! United! United!

United! United! United!   city   city   United! United

United! United! United! United! United! United!

United! United! United! United! United! United!

United! United! United! United! United! United!

Sponsored by Rustbucket Motors

Sponsored by ZAPPUM Insecurity Lights

John Coldwell

Gillingham

33

Riddles

I've got a roof,
A wide front door,
A back door only for small insects,
A strong frame,
And plenty of windows for
people to see through.

I have a bottom right corner
And a top left corner.
I control a box
And I'm good at geometry
Some people say I'm brave
Others say I'm crazy.
I can fly
And prefer my sheets to be clean
Who am I?

The chip spinning like a satellite
Arcs its way with computerised precision
To the striker's head;
To leave him only one decision –
To leave the keeper dead:
One orbit.

Scoring a goal

Goal-keeper

A goal net

Well, these riddles beat me! ...

He starts from the six yard box
Leaves ten astonished faces standing
Leaves eleven even more astonished faces
As he scores.

He takes his job very seriously
Never forgetting his keys.
Every evening after dark,
Come rain, wind or snow
He throws in a couple of old ones,
But on their birthdays,
He treats them to fresh, tasty new ones.

Ian Blackman
Brighton and Hove Albion

Own goal

Goal-keeper

My Team's Not Scoring

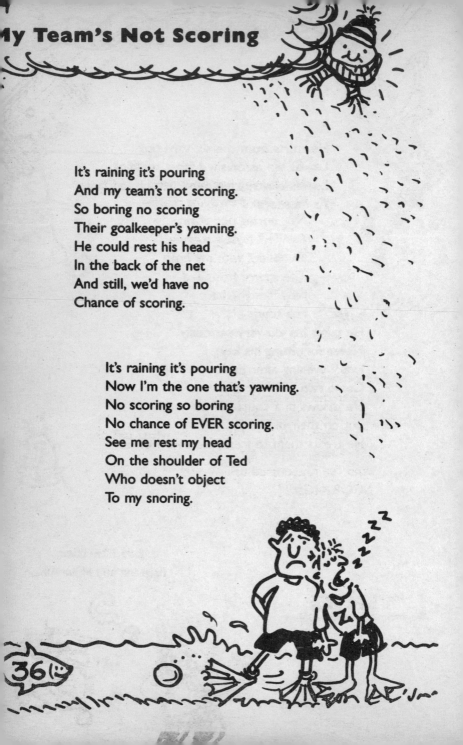

It's raining it's pouring
And my team's not scoring.
So boring no scoring
Their goalkeeper's yawning.
He could rest his head
In the back of the net
And still, we'd have no
Chance of scoring.

It's raining it's pouring
Now I'm the one that's yawning.
No scoring so boring
No chance of EVER scoring.
See me rest my head
On the shoulder of Ted
Who doesn't object
To my snoring.

Not raining nor pouring
Now the crowd are roaring.
Not boring not boring
As I feel myself soaring,
To deflect with my head
The centre from Ted
Now I'm the hero
For scoring.

Not raining nor pouring
I hear the fans applauding.
Not boring I'm scoring
Their faith I am .... what? eh? oh!
It's raining it's pouring
And I've just missed us
SCORING!

Ian Blackman
Brighton and Hove Albion

No Football

The teachers took our ball.
We'd only sent it over the fence
for the seventh time that week!
But Kevin was cheeky to some old boy
who wouldn't give it back.
'That's that,' our headmaster said.
'We'll keep it now for a bit
    until you learn to play properly.'
Kevin tried to tell him that
we couldn't learn to play properly
if we weren't practising,
but he said it was cheek like that
had cost us our ball in the first place.

After that there was nothing to do;
someone lost a shoe and we passed that about,
then made do with half a conker
and put up quite a dazzling display
till Kevin let it slip down a drain,
then took the cover off to get it back.
'You'll take that and yourself to the Head,'
our teacher said. 'And what do you think
you were doing with your arm
down that filthy thing?'

When Kevin came back he grinned and said
we'd lost our ball for good.
We moped around with nothing to kick
till later, behind the teacher's back,
we took it in turns to kick Kevin.

Brian Moses
Tottenham Hotspur

Goalie

I am the most popular player in the team.
I have just pulled off the most brilliant save.
I've got the ball.
My team are yelling and screaming
So.
I bounce it a couple of times,
Then give it an almighty kick
Right up the middle of the pitch.
Let them sort it out.

I am the loneliest player in the team.
There are twenty one players up the other end,
Leaving me down here.
I think we're in possession.
But I don't really care.
I prefer my own company.
It gives me time to think about things –
Like,
Can I touch the cross bar from a standing jump?

I am the most unpopular player in the team.
It wasn't my fault they scored.
I was hanging from the cross bar at the time.
Where was the defence?
That's what I'd like to know.
I can't cover for all their mistakes.

The captain said,
I can't be the goalkeeper
If I let another in.
Suits me.
I didn't want to be in goal anyway.
I'm more of an attacking player.
They need me out on the pitch.
So,
I won't bother to save the next shot.
Then I'll have just enough time
To score a hat trick.

John Coldwell
Gillingham

41

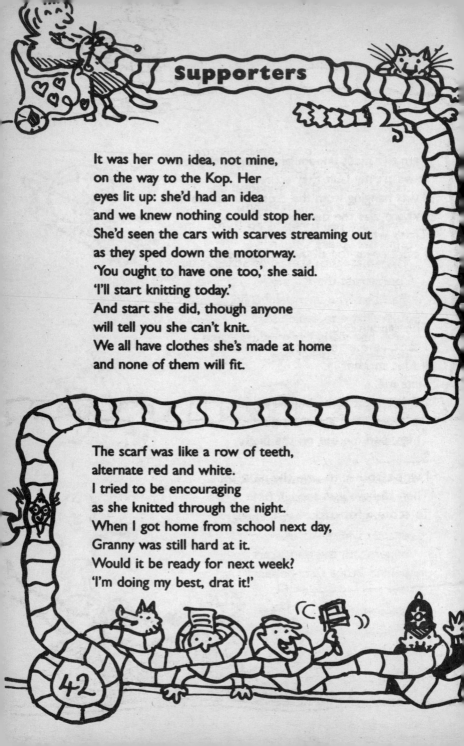

Supporters

It was her own idea, not mine,
on the way to the Kop. Her
eyes lit up: she'd had an idea
and we knew nothing could stop her.
She'd seen the cars with scarves streaming out
as they sped down the motorway.
'You ought to have one too,' she said.
'I'll start knitting today.'
And start she did, though anyone
will tell you she can't knit.
We all have clothes she's made at home
and none of them will fit.

The scarf was like a row of teeth,
alternate red and white.
I tried to be encouraging
as she knitted through the night.
When I got home from school next day,
Granny was still hard at it.
Would it be ready for next week?
'I'm doing my best, drat it!'

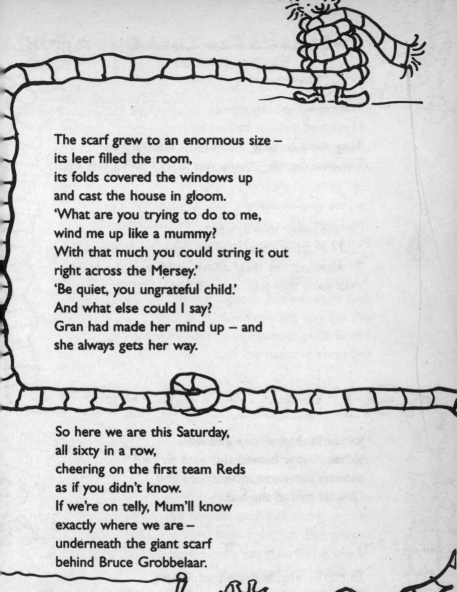

The scarf grew to an enormous size –
its leer filled the room,
its folds covered the windows up
and cast the house in gloom.
'What are you trying to do to me,
wind me up like a mummy?
With that much you could string it out
right across the Mersey.'
'Be quiet, you ungrateful child.'
And what else could I say?
Gran had made her mind up – and
she always gets her way.

So here we are this Saturday,
all sixty in a row,
cheering on the first team Reds
as if you didn't know.
If we're on telly, Mum'll know
exactly where we are –
underneath the giant scarf
behind Bruce Grobbelaar.

Jill Townsend
Liverpool

Wow! ! Let's See That One Again! !

They didn't exactly invite
Marie and Vanessa to join in,
They were hanging around just watching by
The goal mouth — there was Gary's parka one side,

On the other Weedy's bag —
And I imagine when they thought they'd seen enough
To work out for themselves which way the game
Was going they just, sort of,

Joined in. And all of a sudden
When Kipper heaved this pass to Paul,
Vanessa somehow intercepted and
Quickly passed the ball.

To Marie, who at once sent Rabbit
The wrong way, and after dumping Nick
Next she neatly side-stepped
Martin's size 13 Doc

Marten's, then bounced it round Yacko
With just one rebound off the Chemi Lab
Before backheeling to Vanessa who from all of twenty yards
Drove it past Kevin's despairing, diving grab.

Kev winds up with his head in Weedy's bag
And as five out of ten players plus Marie all
Jump excitedly about and punch the air,
He just gets up and trudges off to find the ball.

Then five out of ten players plus   Marie
Run towards the scorer to embrace   and fling
Themselves upon her. And freeze. Just   like the real thing,
Just like they end those replays on TV.

David Horner
Huli City and Warrington Town

45

Ref Rap

Clap clap
Clap clap clap
Clap clap clap clap
Clap clap
I don't win
I don't lose
I point the finger
Uphold the rules
I show the card
I send them off
I blow the whistle
When I've had enough
Clap clap
Clap clap clap
Clap clap clap clap
Clap clap
Fans all chant
Supporters sing
Can't hear the word
I like to think
it's
'We love
We all love
We all love the referee
He's brave
He's strong
His eyesight's great
He's not the man
We love to hate

46   He's the F.C. M.C.

He does
No wrong
He's always right
He's on the ball
He's dynamite
And we love
We all love
We all love the referee'
Clap clap
Clap clap clap
Clap clap clap clap
Clap clap
I don't get dirty
Don't get hurt
In my referee's shorts
In my referee's shirt
It's plain to see
So you must agree
The man to be
Is the referee
Ref ref
Ref ref ref
Ref ref ref ref
Ref ref

peep
peep
peeego!!!

Bernard Young
Manchester United

I ♥ Rave Rovers

47

FA Rules OK

Life isn't easy in our house
My dad's a referee
He's always right, never wrong
And he knows all the rules.

Everyday he comes home
Shiny black shirt
Shiny black shorts
Shiny red face
Shiny silver whistle.

He races around the house
Checking the nets on the curtains
The height of the crossbars over the doors.

He doesn't like it
When the budgie talks back to him
He gets mad when the dog
Dribbles down his leg
And he booked the cat for spitting.

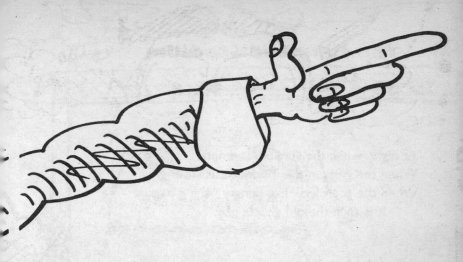

If we don't wash our hands before tea
That's it – a warning.
Leaving our greens – yellow card.
Giving them to the dog – red card.

Being sent off in your own house
Is no fun.
It's a long lonely walk upstairs
For that early bath
Early bed, no telly
And no extra time.

Yes, life isn't easy in our house
Dad's always right
And he knows all the rules.

Paul Cookson and David Harmer
Everton and Sheffield United

tough
lesson
to lea
kid
...do
worry
about
it.

49

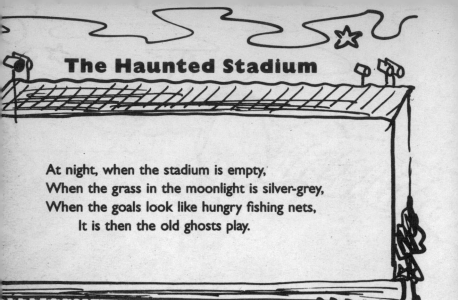

The Haunted Stadium

At night, when the stadium is empty,
When the grass in the moonlight is silver-grey,
When the goals look like hungry fishing nets,
    It is then the old ghosts play.

When all the crisp packets and fag-ends
And the drink cans have been swept up,
And the crowd has left, and the gates are locked,
    They play for the Phantom Cup.

Thin clouds drift across the face of the moon,
The grass stirs, a preeping whistle sounds,
And silent invisible spectators
    Throng the deserted stands.

50

And twenty-two ghosts in long-legged shorts
Dance the ball across the silvered grass,
A ball you can almost see, the old game —
    Run, dribble and pass.

Pale shades and shadows, heroes of bygone days,
Under the gaze of the moon, sidestep and swerve,
And crowds silently cheer as the ball floats
    Goalwards in an unseen curve.

Gerard Benson
    Arsenal

Worm's-Eye-View of the FA Cup Final

'That's funny,' said the worm
as it went under Wembley.
'I wonder why the ground's
so loud and trembly.'

Tony Mitton
Manchester United

Hope you've enjoyed burrowing in this book!

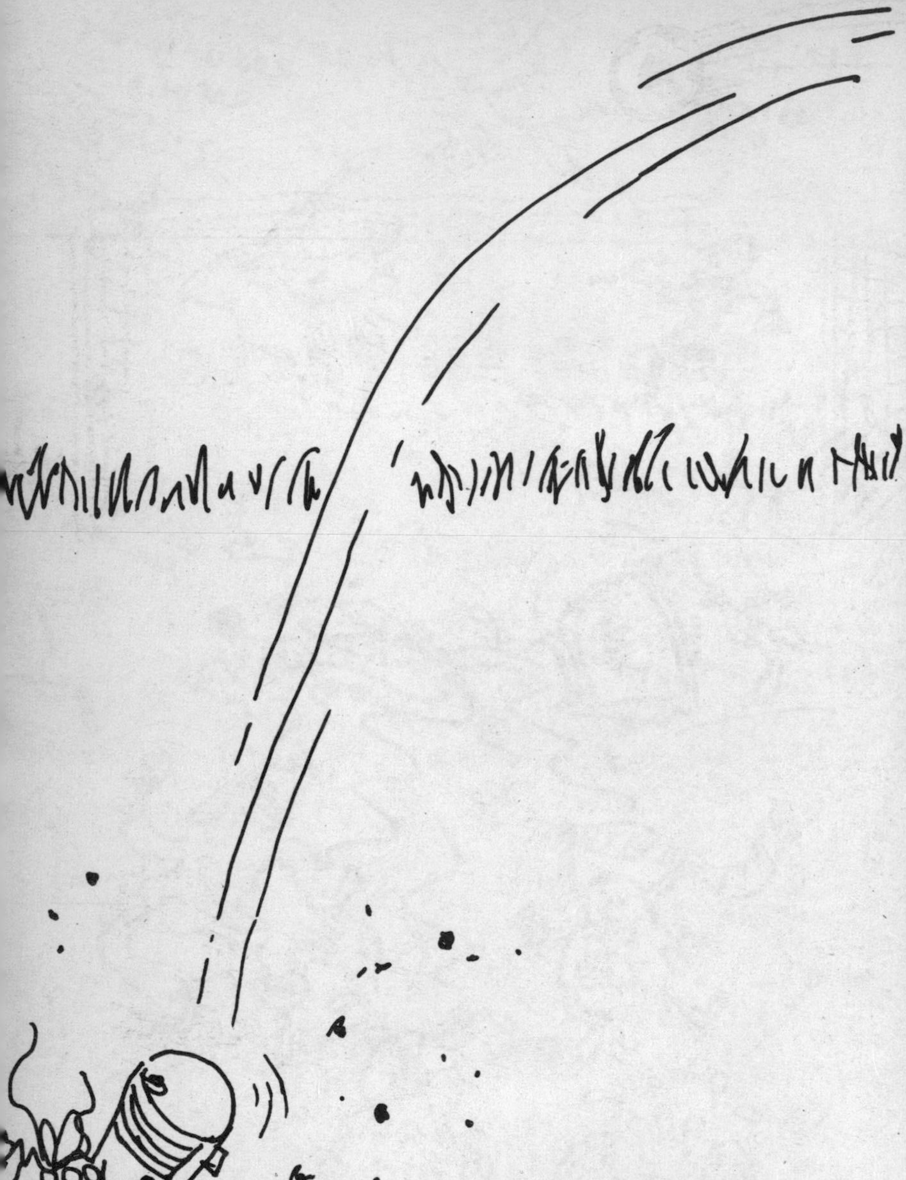

Football Facts

by Ian Blackman

Jargon . . .

Bench Place or seat where the manager, trainer and substitutes sit during game (also called the subs bench).

Box Penalty area.

Checking Moving one way, stopping to move off in another direction.

Chip A pass or attempt at goal made by a stabbing action of the kicking foot to achieve a sharp flight upwards of the ball.

Clean sheet A goalkeeper's ultimate aim of having no goals scored against (also named **Blank sheet**).

Close down To restrict the amount of space available to an opponent.

Cross To play the ball from a wide position, i.e. the wing, into a more central position.

Cushion Controlling the ball by withdrawing the surface contacted by the ball, e.g. pulling back the foot at exact moment of contact to soften the impact by taking the speed from the ball.

Deadball Any situation in which the game stops and is restarted by a free-kick, corner, goal-kick, penalty, etc.

Dribble With the ball, going past and beating one or more opponents.

Dummy Deceiving an opponent into thinking you will play the ball when instead you allow the ball to go past, hopefully, to a team-mate.

Football Facts

Early bath When a player is sent off the referee shows a **red card** (either for two separate incidents – two **yellow cards –** one red – or one major incident). This player takes no further part in the game, so may as well have a bath.

Engine room The midfield, the work-horses, a human dynamo. This position requires enormous amounts of stamina as the midfield must help out in defence as well as supporting the forwards.

Feint A deceptive movement with or without the ball.

Fifty-fifty ball when two players have an equal chance of winning the ball.

Flanks Area of pitch close to each touchline.

Goal-poacher A striker who posesses the natural instinct to 'steal' a chance to score. A top-class **striker** always needs the 'scent' for making something out of nothing.

Half-volley Contact with the ball the exact moment it touches the ground.

Hospital pass When a player's poor pass could cause a team-mate possible injury.

Hustle Putting an opponent under constant pressure.

Long throw A tactic whereby the throw-in is used like a corner, by throwing the ball into the penalty area.

Loose ball when neither side has control or possession of the ball.

Mark(ing) Taking up a position to tackle or deny an opponent possession of the ball.

Football Facts

Man to man marking Marking the same player throughout the match (becoming the player's second skin or shadow).

Nutmeg When the ball passes between the legs.

One-touch Passing the ball first time, i.e. without controlling it.

One-two A quick exchange of passes between two players.

Professional foul If there is a good scoring opportunity and the attacker is deliberately fouled. This **usually** warrants a red card without warning.

Red card The equivalent of two **yellow cards** really. A bookable offence. You're off!

Set-up (on a plate) Such an easy chance that even you or I could score with our eyes closed!

Striker Attacking player whose main job is to score lots of goals.

Sweeper A defender who is spare at the back and can read the game so any danger can be anticipated. Can also be an attacking player by bringing the ball out of defence.

Wall (building a) A defensive barrier formed by players to block a free-kick near goal. The goalkeeper dictates how many players are needed to make up the wall.

Whistle-happy referee An official who spoils the flow of the game by continually stopping the action for fussy reasons.

Yellow card First caution. In effect, a warning.

The Dream Team

Franz Beckenbauer BAYERN MUNICH and WEST GERMANY. On the 8 July 1990 he became the only man to have both captained and managed a World Cup winning nation (as a player he won a Winner's Medal in 1974). Formally a midfield player he switched to become a world-class sweeper and was his country's most effective attacking player. He acted very coolly under pressure.

George Best MANCHESTER UNITED and NORTHERN IRELAND. Won two League Championship medals and finally, in 1968, the European Cup. A tricky winger with a completely individual style. A great entertainer and brilliant dribbler with tremendous balance, which enabled him to go round or ride opponents' tackles or challenges as he twisted and turned his way to goal.

Bobby Charlton MANCHESTER UNITED and ENGLAND. The complete footballer possessing a marvellous pass, surging power and a cannonball shot. Won Winner's Medals in the FA Cup, League Championship, and European Cup. Capped 106 times for his country, scoring 49 goals, and helped England win the World Cup in 1966. A perfect ambassador for football.

Paul Gascoigne NEWCASTLE, SPURS, LAZIO and ENGLAND. A Geordie who left English football when he transferred to the Italian side Lazio for £5 million. His rise to stardom was due not to luck but to his eagerness to learn and practise his skills. Gazza's remarkable energy and willingness to succeed helped him shine during the 1990 World Cup Finals in Italy. Although no one player is bigger than the team, he is the type of player any manager would love to build a team around.

The Dream Team

Diego Maradona BARCELONA, NAPOLI and ARGENTINA. First played for his country at seventeen when he came on as a substitute. Helped Napoli win two Italian championships. At his peak he was said to be the world's best dribbler. Strong, with good balance, he had electrifying pace over the first five metres. He terrified defences by running directly at them. Banned from football in 1991 for a year after failing a dope test. Now playing in Spanish league for Sevilla.

Sir Stanley Matthews STOKE, BLACKPOOL and ENGLAND. League début in 1932 at seventeen and last league game at the age of fifty. Supremely fit and a perfect gentleman on and off the field. First footballer to be knighted whilst still playing. Neat and tricky winger whose skills brought crowds to their feet wherever he played. Finally won an FA Cup Winner's Medal at the age of thirty-eight with Blackpool. Won the last of his 54 England caps aged forty-two. The first European Footballer of the Year.

Bobby Moore WEST HAM UNITED and ENGLAND. A world-class defender whose coolness, vision and passing created many goals. England's youngest ever captain at twenty-four, he was capped 108 times for his country. In the sixties he captained West Ham to FA Cup and European Cup Winners Cup success. He also captained England to their only World Cup success, beating West Germany 4–2 in 1966. A true sportsman and gentleman, sadly he died of cancer in 1993 aged fifty-one.

Pele SANTOS and BRAZIL. While still a teenager (seventeen) he scored two goals in the 1958 World Cup Final triumph over Sweden. One of his goals is said, by many, to be the greatest goal ever scored in a World Cup Final; Pele took a high ball on his thigh, hooked it over his head, spinning round, he volleyed the ball into the Swedish net. Won the World Cup again with

The Dream Team

Brazil in 1970. Regarded by many as the best ever footballer, he averaged almost a goal a game – during a career which spanned about 1200 games. A true entertainer with beautiful silky skills and the ability to create the unexpected.

Ferenc Puskas HONVED, REAL MADRID and HUNGARY. He possessed a thunderbolt left foot and had brilliant vision for a pass or a shot. In 1958 he signed for Real Madrid, receiving a £10,000 signing-on fee. Retired in 1966 and as manager took the Greek champions Panethinaikos to a European Cup Final.

Marco Van Basten AJAX, AC MILAN and HOLLAND. The best striker in the world today. Voted European Fooballer of the Year in 1992 for third time in his career. Father was a footballer, mother was a world-class athlete. Signed for Dutch club Ajax at sixteen. Scored 128 goals, averaging almost one a game. In the 1985–86 season he won the coveted golden Boot Award, scoring 37 goals in 26 league games. The following season he scored 31, and captained Ajax to a Cup Winners Cup victory. Transferred to Italian side AC Milan and was top scorer in the 1991–92 Italian league, winning the championship unbeaten. Also won the European Nations Cup with Holland.

Lev Yashin MOSCOW DYNAMO and RUSSIA. European Footballer of the Year 1963. Before making the first team he nearly gave up the game in favour of ice hockey. He was not only famous for his acrobatic displays in goals, but for his great sportsmanship. Whilst playing for The Rest of the World Team v England at Wembley, a scorching shot soared towards his goal – the only part of his body that moved was one arm as he jabbed out a fist to punch the ball away for a throw-in.

So You Want to be a Professional Footballer?

One You must have ability. This ability can be encouraged and developed by a parent, a relation, a friend, a teacher, or an organiser of an out-of-school club.

Two Football must be in your blood. To succeed you will need to eat, drink and sleep football. Dedication and the willingness to learn are vital.

Three Represent your school team.

Four Represent your district team.

Five Represent your county team.

Six Be invited to attend schoolboy trials at a full-time professional club. Be recommended to a club by your team manager or teacher.

Seven Be offered a schoolboy apprenticeship. Play for club's youth team, then progress to reserve team football.

Eight Be offered a full-time adult apprenticeship.

Nine First team début: your future at your feet, and in your head and heart.

Ten Alternatively you could be out playing semi-professional part-time football or Sunday football and, watching from the touchline, is a scout. He spots your talent and you are plucked from obscurity into the 'big time'. Keep dreaming, for dreams can come true.

YOU'LL NEVER WALK ALONE

Contents

Extra Time: Football Facts

Worm's-Eye-View of
the Replay at Wembley

What's that pattering?
Can it be rain?
Oh no — a re-play!
'Ere we go again . . .

Tony Mitton
Manchester United

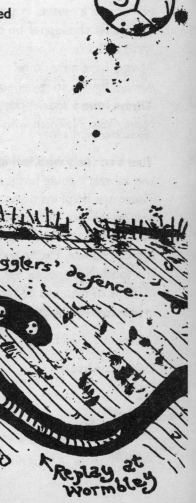

. . . as 'e swerves past
Wormberhampton Wigglers' defence . . .

↑ Replay at
Wormbley

Catch of the Day's Shoal of the Season

Always choose an octopus for goalie
Always have a whale for the defensive wall
Always have a salmon for high crosses
Never let a swordfish head the ball at all.

Never make an enemy of a sea anemone
Never have a clash with a giant clam
Never pull a mussel in a tackle or a tussle
Always let the kipper be the skipper if you can.

Always have a mackerel to tackle well
Always have a sting-ray staying on the wing
Always have a shark – he's an expert at attack
Never kiss a jellyfish who scores with a sting.

There are eels who feel electric playing at a pace that's hectic
and lobster's going potty scoring from an indirect kick.
There are dolphins doing dribbling weaving round shoals,
helping whelks, out-thinking winkles, getting lots of goals.

Mediterranean, Pacific and Atlantic
the football is specific yet very very frantic.
Millions of matches of varying degrees
in the twenty thousand leagues under the seas.

Paul Cookson
Everton

can I 'av me ball back?

Goal!

An excitement spark
A net bulger
A keep distresser
A seat spring
A defender incenser
A manager's grin-maker
A trainer jumper
A scoreboard changer
A crowd maddener
A glory glory spreader
A team promoter
A game finisher
A fun-journey-home-maker.

Daniel Sedgwick
Ipswich Town

We Cannot Lose Again!

Here we go and here we go
and here we go again
hoping that today our brilliant team
will reach its peak.
Last Saturday was dreadful,
our defence just looked so weak,
but now it's our turn to be lucky,
for we cannot lose again!

Here we go and here we go
and here we go again –
we cannot get the stupid ball
stuck into their net
and they're looking deadly
when they break out quickly, yet
it's our turn to be lucky,
for we cannot lose again!
Here we go and here we go

and here we go again
wishing we'd gone and done
some shopping in the town,
but we mustn't give up easily,
we're only one goal down
and it's our turn to be lucky,
for we cannot lose again!

Here we go and here we go
and here we go again
leaving after losing,
our position's looking bleak.
Yet all of us will congregate
to cheer them on next week
when it's our turn to be lucky,
for we cannot lose again!

Peter Comaish
Liverpool

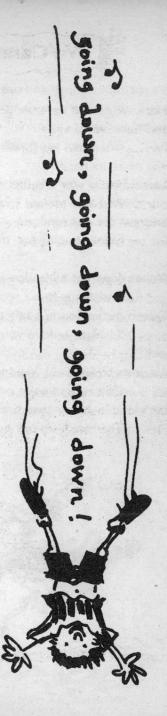

A Perfect Match

We met in Nottingham Forest,
  My sweet Airdrie and I.
She smiled and said, 'Alloa!' to me –
  Oh, never say goodbye!

I asked her, 'Is your Motherwell?'
  And she replied, 'I fear
She's got the Academicals
  From drinking too much beer.'

We sat down on a Meadowbank
  And of my love I spoke.
'Queen of the South,' I said to her,
  'My fires of love you Stoke!'

We went to Sheffield, Wednesday.
  Our Hearts were one. Said she:
'Let's wed in Accrington, Stanley,
  Then we'll United be.'

The ring was Stirling silver,
      Our friends, Forfar and wide,
A motley Crewe, all gathered there
      and fought to kiss the bride.

The best man had an awful lisp.
      'Come Raith your glatheth up,'
He said, and each man raised on high
      His Coca-Cola cup.

The honeymoon was spent abroad:
      We flew out east by Ayr,
And found the far-off Orient
      Partick-ularly fair.

We're home, in our own Villa now,
      (The Walsall painted grey)
And on our Chesterfield we sit
      And watch Match of the Day.

Pam Gidney
Chelsea

Tell Me About Your Dream

'Well
It's always the same you see
Never varies
And always leaves me sweating with fright.
Talk you through it?
Well, I'll try.

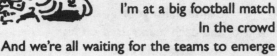

I'm at a big football match
In the crowd
And we're all waiting for the teams to emerge
When suddenly over the speakers
This voice comes
Very loud and very clear
And I get the feeling
It's speaking to me.

Do I remember what it says?
Well yes:
Two players have missed the coach
So they're a man short.
If anybody happens
To have their boots on them
They'd be grateful if he'd play.
What?
Of course I've got my boots
Because I know from my dream
That this may happen.
That's right
I don't know if it's a dream or not.
In a flash
I'm over the barrier
And in the dressing-rooms.
Suddenly famous players
Are shaking my hand

And clapping me on the back.
As we set off down the tunnel
The manager puts his hand on my arm.
He looks me in the eye and says,
"Take the number 9 shirt lad
Wear it with pride lad
You're captain for the day."

And then I'm off
Up the dark tunnel
To a green field called Glory.
My studs rattle on the concrete
And the roar of the crowd
Is like a great beast breathing
Far away.
Breathing my name over and over.
I come to a wall.

I don't know whether to go left or right.
I take the right one
But the right one
Turns out to be the wrong one.
It leads to another corridor
And another
And another
And another.
The beast has stopped breathing now
I call out
But my voice
Comes back off the endless white walls.

Then I wake up
Sweating and shaking with fright.
Well that's it.
Has it helped to talk about it?
Well, yes I suppose it has.
Do I want to ask any questions?

Miracles Can Happen

Dad stomped in, all grumpy and sore,
He stamped his feet and slammed the door.
He growled and grimaced and threw down his coat,
And made funny noises down in his throat.
Then Mum said kindly, 'Don't worry dear –
United might still win a game this year . . .'

Samson United

They're the strongest team in the league –
Not because they're the best,
But because they're stuck at the bottom
And have to prop up the rest . . .

Dead Cert

After missing his umpteenth penalty,
'I could kick myself,' he said.
'I wouldn't bother, you'd only miss,'
Muttered poor old manager Fred.

Clive Webster
Sheffield United

Wilmington Wanderers' Weekly Wash

Eleven shirts, eleven shorts, twenty-one socks . . .
Twenty-one socks? Where's the one that got away?
Eleven shirts, eleven shorts, twenty-TWO socks
Went whirling round in the washer window.

I'll have to find a substitute – a transfer from the Cubs?
It's not exactly 'Strip' I know, but with a bit of luck,
Nobody'll notice the lack of navy stripes.

Eleven shirts, eleven shorts, twenty-TWO socks
Whirled round that washer window.
The power-packed powder pounded the stains
(The packet said it removed the most stubborn).
Perhaps that sock was all dirt!

Catherine Benson
Wilmington Wanderers and
Bradford City

...2..3...4...5..

... Feed the machine more socks!

18

Nightplayer

My dad's mad about football.
He even plays it in his dreams.
My mum doesn't mind that much,
But the whistle makes her scream.

Janis Priestley
Aston Villa

Football on the Brain

In the yard at ten to nine.
In the yard at break.
On the field at dinner-time
until our legs all ache.

Out there when it's cold and hard.
Out there in the rain.
That's the way with our lot:
Football on the brain.

Some like playing marbles.
Some like games of chase.
Some just like to muck about
and stand around the place.

But our lot run together
with passes swift and neat.
Out lot's always on the move,
a football at our feet.

Some say, 'I'd get tired.'
Some say, 'I'd get bored.'
But they don't know the buzz you get
when you're the one that's scored.

Some say, 'Why the trouble?'
Some say, 'What's the fuss?'
But our lot's off to Wembley.
That's the place for us.

Out there when it's cold and hard.
Out there in the rain.
That's the way with our lot:
Football on the brain.

Tony Mitton
Manchester United

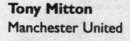

Football!

Football! *Football!*
The boys want the *entire* playground
and we're left squashed
against the broken fence.
Why don't the teachers stop them?
Why?
Haven't they got *any* sense?

My friend Anna
ran across the tarmac.

Smack!
Got the football right on her nose.
Blood all over her face.
Why don't the teachers do something?
Why?
It's a disgrace, a disgrace!

Those boys . . . I mean
they're like hooligans.
CHEL-SEA! CHEL-SEA! they chant
morning, noon and night.
The teacher on duty does . . . nothing.
Why?
It's just . . . it's just not right!

We complain bitterly
but the duty teacher says,
'Go and see the Head. He's in charge.'
Him! He's *useless!* YOU-ESS-LESS!
When we ask him to ban football
why,
oh why, can't he just say 'Yes'?

Wes Magee
Swindon Town

Out of the Cup

An open goal, lad, a gaping, can't-miss goal!
A banged-in, dead-cert, asking-for-it goal!
Talk about butter-fingers — we'll have to call you
butter-boots! What d'you do? Smear Kerrygold on them?

All you had to do was tap it in, a simple tap,
a toe-cap tap. But no! you had to dash at it,
to rush at it, to take a mighty swipe at it.
I'm not the only one

who wished to hear a solid thud, a spot-on thud,
dead-centre-of-the-ball and cheer-your-lungs-out,
go-down-in-history, kick-of-the-century thud.

A goal! A know-you've-won, a blinder goal. And NOT
a try-again-next-season shot.

Matt Simpson
Liverpool

Billy Jenkins

Billy Jenkins doesn't come to school
every day. He's in a wheelchair.
Sometimes he has to go to the hospital.

He likes football. When the weather's dry
he comes out to support the team.
He wears a tartan rug over his knees.

He lives in the house by the post-box,
the one with the big garden and all the trees.
He sits outside in summer and watches people.

I had a dream about him. It was a Saturday.
Billy Jenkins jumped out of his wheelchair
and ran down the road, kicking a football.

We were all shouting as he passed the full-back
and closed in on the goalie. He scored with ease,
as we waved our tartan rugs in the air.

Tony Charles
Wolverhampton
Wanderers

go Billy!

The Penalty

If I place it to his left
    Will he guess wrong?

        If I place it to his right
            Will he guess right?

I'll look to his right
    And place it left

        Or should I look to his left
          And place it right?

No, I'll shape up right
    And hit it right.

            Or should I . . . ?

Ian Blackman
Brighton and Hove Albion

25

Can I av me ball back?

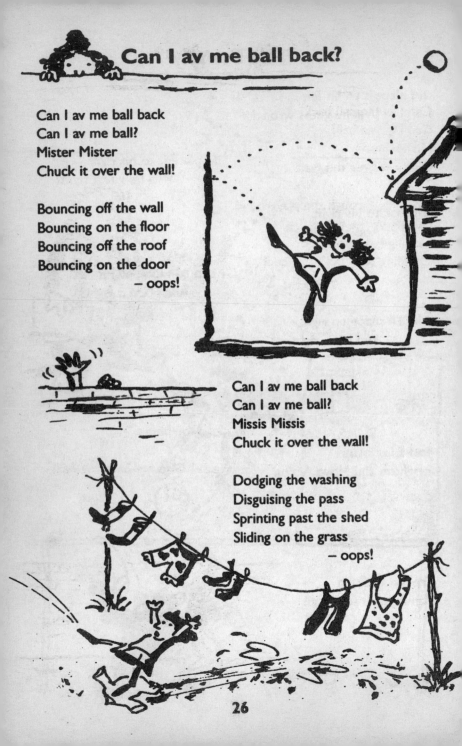

Can I av me ball back
Can I av me ball?
Mister Mister
Chuck it over the wall!

Bouncing off the wall
Bouncing on the floor
Bouncing off the roof
Bouncing on the door
           – oops!

Can I av me ball back
Can I av me ball?
Missis Missis
Chuck it over the wall!

Dodging the washing
Disguising the pass
Sprinting past the shed
Sliding on the grass
           – oops!

Can I av me ball back
Can I av me ball?
Mister Mister
Chuck it over the wall!

Storming through the playground
Gliding by the flower bed
Leaping in the corridor
Colliding with the . . . Head!
     – oops!

Staring at the ceiling . . .
Staring at the wall . . .
Oh, keep me in for hours
But

  – Please! Give me back me ball!

Trevor Millum
Hamilton Academicals

Overheard in the Changing-room

Scoring goals,
That's all they want to hear about!
The swing; the thump;
The leather speeding into the net!

But that's rubbish. It's all rubbish.
Scoring is easy for any well-made boot.
What about the running?
(Oh not like your ordinary
boot or shoe).
The dancing!
The skipping sideways!
The sudden dazzling changes of direction!
They are the business.

> *Said the old left boot*
> *In the corner of the changing-room,*
> *His voice so quiet,*
> *A whisper in the gloom.*

Goals? Nothing! Crash, bang, wallop
And back to the spot.
But the dancing! Imagine.
Tip-tapping the ball,
Inside the foot, outside,
Toecap, instep, heel.
Can you? Can you imagine it?
Swivelling, shuffling,
Not too fast, then checking,
And only then the sudden dash . . .
The sure-footed surge of speed.
Those are the delights:

> *An old left boot*
> *Slung in the corner*
> *Amid the shirts and shorts*
> *Whispering – 'Goals? Nothing.'*

Although . . .
Although to tap it,
To screw it,
To trickle it,
To slot it,
To slice it,
To lob it,
To swerve it,
To drift it,
To drive it
Past those outstretched hands –
There was pleasure in that.

> *Last season's boot*
> *Chucked in the corner,*
> *Muttering*
> *Mumbling away.*

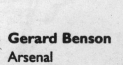

Gerard Benson
Arsenal

Pre-match Rap

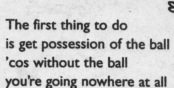

The first thing to do
is get possession of the ball
'cos without the ball
you're going nowhere at all

work it from the back
build it up real slow
no back passing
there's only one way to go

take it down the middle
or send it out wide
just make sure you don't
give it the opposing side

when you get to the box
knock it on through
try to penetrate
with a quick one-two

with close control
work that ball
carry it past
their defensive wall

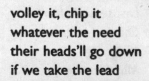

volley it, chip it
whatever the need
their heads'll go down
if we take the lead

give it what you've got
body and soul
whatever you do
just go for goal

and come the final whistle
you'll have the fame you seek
absolute heroes
till the same time next week

now let's get out there and do the business!

Tony Langham
Bolton Wanderers

Losing Marker

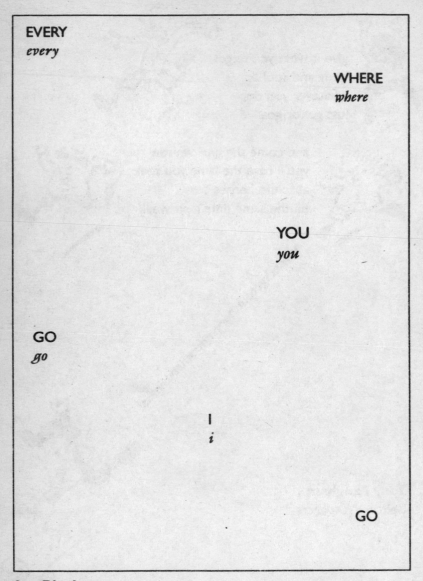

EVERY
every

WHERE
where

YOU
you

GO
go

I
i

GO

Ian Blackman
Brighton and Hove Albion

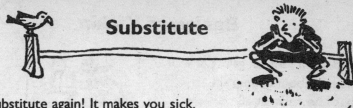

Substitute

Not substitute again! It makes you sick.
It wouldn't matter if we sometimes won
but we're one down, and taking lots of stick.
It was same last Saturday: 4–1.

Why is it that the Coach will never pick
me for the team? I don't know what I've done.
What's that he's saying now? Go on for Mick
who's hurt his leg? Great! This should be more fun.

The linesman nods: I'm on. I get a kick.
Then Barry passes, Raj goes on a run.
His marker tackles but Raj is too quick:
he floats a lovely ball into the sun.
I head it down. Now – it's just one to one.
And I am past the keeper. Yes! 1–1!

Jill Townsend
Liverpool

Backyard Kickin

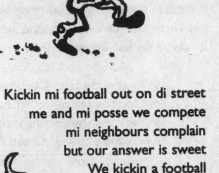

Kickin mi football gainst di wall
mi neighbours complain
but I no harm at all
kickin mi football
dat's all!

Kickin mi football out on di street
me and mi posse we compete
mi neighbours complain
but our answer is sweet
We kickin a football
dat's all!

Dad kick mi football at di weekend
Kickin so hard he pretend
he really de boss o' England!
Mi neighbours complain
they gotta window to mend
cos Dad kick mi football
over di wall.

  Dat's all.

Chris Riley
Italy

34

Match Report

So there's just ten minutes left
right and Benson says okay you're
on right just like that right no
warning or anything like that and
I say what position sir right and
he says on the right right so I go
on right and as soon as we get
started Degsey bangs one over to me
right and I leg it right down to
the corner flag and knock one over
right and Billy Khan's right there
deadcentre and he hits it just right
and it goes right in sweetasanut

Tony Langham
Bolton Wanderers

The Best Match of the Year

Did you see it?
Did *you* see it?

Lee's brilliant shot, from way outside the box:

WOOOSH!

Top left-hand corner of the net;
their goalie had NO CHANCE.

Did you see it?
Did *you* see it?

But what about . . . but what about our keeper's

SUPERSAVE

just before half-time?
Old glue-gloves held on to it.

Did you see it?
Did *you* see it?

Wow! Cor! Phew, I'll never forget those two

CRUNCHING

tackles by Big Chris;
crucial, I mean K-Roo-Shul.

Did you see it?
Did *you* see it?

No, neither did I.

Mike Johnson
Blackburn Rovers

36

Why Groundsmen Never Relax

We're the touchy ones who patch up the pitches
when the action of each game dispatches grass patches
and batches of scratch-marks, where boots catch, carve ditches.
We're grouches because of such hitches.
We've a hotch-potch of blotches, a richness of itches,
much agony, ouches and stitches,
all actually brought on by these glitches
due to passes and tackles and switches.
And it's match-watching which is
what hatches our unnatural twitches.

Nick Toczek
Bradford

The Football Pitch is Waterlogged

The football pitch is waterlogged
the grass is like an ocean.
Because of all the rain and mud
everything's slow motion.

The full-back's wearing flippers
instead of football boots
and tracksuits have been replaced
by frogmen's diving suits.

The wingers have got waders,
the left one – a life jacket
the right one – a red pacamac
from a plastic packet.

The centre-forward's snorkelling
and wearing water-wings.
There are linesmen on the Lilos
and the ref has rubber rings.

The sweeper sails a speedboat
that has a big propeller.
The manager's not managing
to keep up his umbrella.

The sub's the latest signing
and the sub's a submarine
so the skipper tries to find the ball
in the radar screen.

The goalie has an aqualung
and a periscope
searching to save shots from strikers
striking from U-boats.

The football pitch is waterlogged
with all the players wishing
that their tackles were as useful
as the tackle used for fishing.

Yes, the football pitch is waterlogged
it's like the English Channel
and as the league's under the sea
we'll need the new Pool's Panel.

There's no sign of any goals scored
just a splash splosh splish
and the only nets they find
are the ones that catch the fish.

Paul Cookson
Everton

Football Word Bank

rank outsiders
everybody behind the ball
got their act together
for a good result
crucial save
turned the game round
man of the match
showed character
played in the right spirit
came back at the end
did the job right
no losers in this game
an amazing turnaround
tactics on the day were right
a fantastic triumph
retired to lick their wounds
wrapped it all up
on the day
the best team
came out on top
a bit lucky in the end

Rita Ray
Manchester City

MR. WISE · AFTER · THE · EVENT

Football Story

This is the foot.

This is the foot
That kicked the ball.

This is the foot
That kicked the ball
That scored the goal.

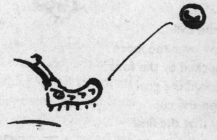

This is the foot
That kicked the ball
That scored the goal
That won the cup.

This is the foot
That kicked the ball
That scored the goal
That won the cup
The day that the final
Was played in our yard.

This is the ball.

This is the ball
That was kicked by the foot
That scored the goal
That won the cup
The day that the final
Was played in our yard.

This is the ball
That flew over the fence
When kicked by the foot
That scored the goal
That won the cup
The day that the final
Was played in our yard.

This is the ball
That flew over the fence
And smashed the window
Of next-door's kitchen
When kicked by the foot
That scored the goal
That won the cup
The day that the final
Was played in our yard.

This is the boy.

This is the boy
Who ran away.

This is the boy
Who ran away
To hide in the shed
When he heard the crash
Made by the ball
That flew over the fence
And smashed the window
Of next-door's kitchen

When kicked by the foot
That scored the goal
That won the cup
The day that the final
Was played in our yard.

This is the father.

This is the father
Who found the boy
Who ran away
To hide in the shed
When he heard the crash
Made by the ball
That flew over the fence
And smashed the window
Of next-door's kitchen
When kicked by the foot
That scored the goal
That won the cup
The day that the final
Was played in our yard.

This is the father
Who dragged home the boy
Who ran away
When he heard the crash
Made by the ball
That flew over the fence
And smashed the window
Of next-door's kitchen
When kicked by the foot
That scored the goal
That won the cup
The day that the final
Was played in our yard.

This is the hand.

This is the hand
Of the father
Who dragged home the boy
Who ran away
When he heard the crash
Made by the ball
That flew over the fence
And smashed the window
Of next-door's kitchen
When kicked by the foot
That scored the goal
That won the cup
The day that the final
Was played in our yard.

This is the hand
Of the father
Who spanked the boy
Who ran away
When he heard the crash
Made by the ball
That flew over the fence
And smashed the window
Of next-door's kitchen
When kicked by the foot
That scored the goal
That won the cup
The day that the final
Was played in our yard.

And this is the boy
Who can't sit down.

John Foster
Carlisle United

Here Are Some Late Football Results

(These matches all kicked off at half past a quarter to)

Back to the Future	3	Batman	2
BBC	2	Channel	4
Who're you waiting	4	Would anyone like an After	8
Frank Bruno hits 'em for	6	Enid Blyton's Famous	5
U	2	Me	2
The Magnificent	7	The Secret	7
Rocky	4	Home Alone	2
All my friends have got	1	I Want one	2
It's Top of the Pops – it's This Week's Number	1	Rambo	3
But Mum why do I have	2	Red Dwarf	6
Jaws	5	Wayne's World	2
You're looki-	0	I'm feeli-	0

David Horner
Hull City and Warrington Town

Will it Go to a Replay?

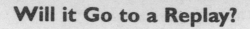

Last night's cup-tie
West Ham and Sheffield United
was so exciting, really tough.

Two teams battled it out
through the rain and mud
as goal after goal
thudded into the net.

The crowd went wild
just loved
every nail-biting moment.

Four–four
with five minutes left
of extra time
both teams down to nine men
and the tension tightening.

In those dying minutes
both sides
cleared their goal lines
with desperate headers.

West Ham missed a penalty
United missed an open goal.

With seconds to go
a replay at Bramall Lane
seemed certain, until

West Ham had to go in for her tea
and Sheffield United went to the shops
for his mum.

David Harmer
Sheffield United

'Ard 'Ead

A tenacious young striker named 'Nutty' McAull
In training one day was headbutting a wall
When quizzed why he did it
'e said 'Obvious, innit –
I 'ate gettin' 'eadaches from 'eadin' a ball!'

Ian Blackman
Brighton and Hove Albion

Dinner-time

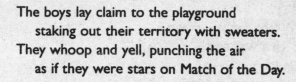

The boys lay claim to the playground
    staking out their territory with sweaters.
They whoop and yell, punching the air
    as if they were stars on Match of the Day.

The girls huddle to one side, clapping rhythms,
skipping rhymes, hop-scotching their time.

Dinner ladies like Sumo wrestlers stand guard.

The Infants steer clear and wonder when
    their mums will come to take them home.

A lone teacher hugs her coffee mug,
    shrugs off the wind and casts a watchful eye.

Other kids gather in corners to swap
    bubble gum cards
        and jokes
            they don't understand.

Pie Corbett
Arsenal

Sideline

Nab that ball!
Steady on!
Don't let Wilson get you down.
Ooooops! That was nasty
– never mind,
it's only mud on your behind.
Come on captain,
make a break
Ouch! * * * * *
Don't start crying for heaven's sake!
It's just a scratch,
that's just a bruise.
We'll treat it later with ice-cubes.
It's only blood that's on your face . . .
Watch out!
Quick, quick, get into place!
Run! Run! Don't stop,
don't look around.
Don't mind that Wilson on the ground.
Kick, quick, kick! kick!
You'll do it yet.
You did! It's in!
It's in the net!
We've won! We've won!
It's all a dream,
and my mum's captain
           of
                   the
                         team!!!

Una Leavy
Manchester United

52

Ere We Go

Ere we go
No fear of foe
Football fans
In frost and snow

Football fans
In fire or flood
In gales that blow,
The truest blood.

Support em high
Support em low
Always Yes
And never No
Ere we, ere we, ere we go.

John Kitching
Sheffield Wednesday

Football

Facts

walk alone !

Twenty Things Needed for a Game of Football in the Local Park

1. Even number of players with at least four wearing anoraks or duffel-coats.

2. Remove anoraks or duffel-coats to use as goal posts.

3. Pick teams.

4. Do not pick smallest or fattest ones last.

5. Get out ball.

6. Argue with each other as to whose turn it is to bring ball.

7. Borrow friend's bike to go home and fetch ball.

8. Meanwhile practise the art of spitting and clearing nose.

9. Get out ball.

10. Argue with person who got ball as to why ball is flat.

11. Borrow another friend's bike to fetch pump.

12. Meanwhile practise rude words to shout at non-existent referee.

13. Pump up ball.

14   Kick off and start game.

15   Commentate like John Motson on passing movements and eventual shot.

16   Argue whether shot
        a) missed
        b) went in
        c) went over anorak post
        d) would have hit post and (i) gone in
                                      (ii) bounced out

17   Try to retrieve ball from muddy ditch behind goals.

18   Do not head ball for at least fifteen minutes.

19   Get jeans as dirty as possible because the dirtier they are the better you must have played.

20   Play until
        a) everyone goes home
        b) it is too dark to see
        c) you are winning
        d) you are winning, it is too dark to see and it is your ball anyway so you're going home.

Paul Cookson
Everton

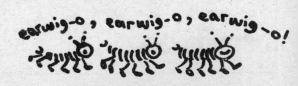
earwig-o, earwig-o, earwig-o!

How to Line Up Your Team

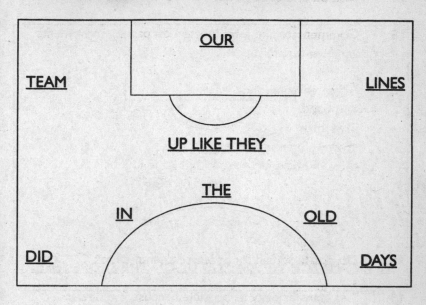

OUR

TEAM · LINES

UP LIKE THEY

THE

IN · OLD

DID · DAYS

FOR
THIS GAME WE ALL
CON CEN TRATE
ON DE FENCE

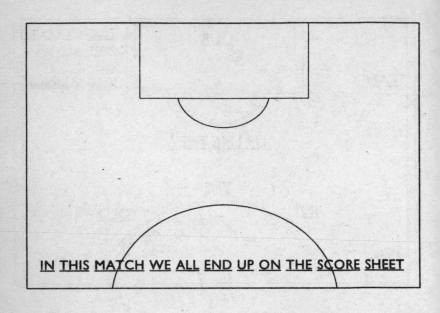

IN THIS MATCH WE ALL END UP ON THE SCORE SHEET

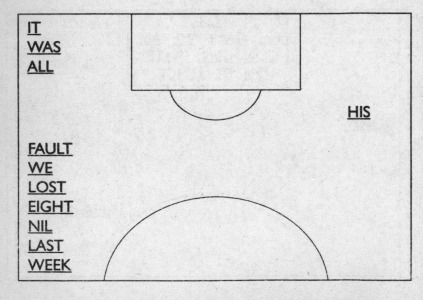

IT
WAS
ALL

HIS

FAULT
WE
LOST
EIGHT
NIL
LAST
WEEK

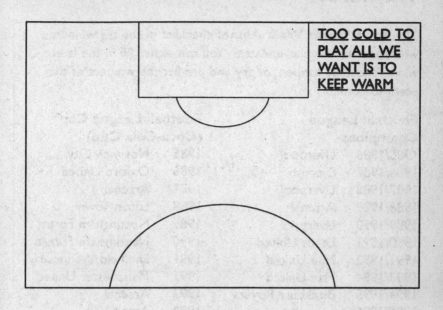

TOO COLD TO PLAY ALL WE WANT IS TO KEEP WARM

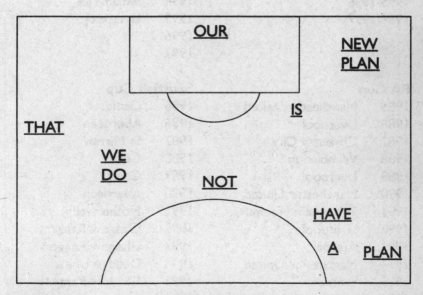

OUR

NEW PLAN

IS

THAT

WE DO

NOT

HAVE

A PLAN

John Coldwell Gillingham

61

Winners!

The **You'll Never Walk Alone!** checklist of the big winners, with space for regular updates! You can either fill in the latest winners as they happen, or try and predict the winners of the years to come!

Football League Champions

1985/1986	Liverpool
1986/1987	Everton
1987/1988	Liverpool
1988/1989	Arsenal
1989/1990	Liverpool
1990/1991	Leeds United
1991/1992	Man United
1993/1994	Man United
1994/1995	Blackburn Rovers
1995/1996	
1996/1997	

Football League Cup (Coca-Cola Cup)

1985	Norwich City
1986	Oxford United
1987	Arsenal
1988	Luton Town
1989	Nottingham Forest
1990	Nottingham Forest
1991	Sheffield Wednesday
1992	Manchester United
1993	Arsenal
1994	Aston Villa
1995	Liverpool
1996	
1997	

FA Cup

1985	Manchester United
1986	Liverpool
1987	Coventry City
1988	Wimbledon
1989	Liverpool
1990	Manchester United
1991	Tottenham Hotspur
1992	Liverpool
1993	Arsenal
1994	Manchester United
1995	Everton
1996	
1997	

Scottish Cup

1985	Celtic
1986	Aberdeen
1987	St Mirren
1988	Celtic
1989	Celtic
1990	Aberdeen
1991	Motherwell
1992	Glasgow Rangers
1993	Glasgow Rangers
1994	Dundee United
1995	Glasgow Rangers
1996	
1997	

Scottish League Champions

1985/1986	Celtic
1986/1987	Glasgow Rangers
1987/1988	Celtic
1988/1989	Glasgow Rangers
1989/1990	Glasgow Rangers
1990/1991	Glasgow Rangers
1991/1992	Glasgow Rangers
1993/1994	Glasgow Rangers
1994/1995	Glasgow Rangers
1995/1996	
1996/1997	

Scottish League Cup

1985/1986	Aberdeen
1986/1987	Glasgow Rangers
1987/1988	Glasgow Rangers
1988/1989	Glasgow Rangers
1989/1990	Aberdeen
1990/1991	Glasgow Rangers
1991/1992	Hibernian
1993/1994	Glasgow Rangers
1994/1995	Glasgow Rangers
1995/1996	
1996/1997	

European Cup

1985	Juventus
1986	Steaua Bucharest
1987	Porto
1988	PSV Eindhoven
1989	AC Milan
1990	AC Milan
1991	Red Star Belgrade
1992	Barcelona
1993	Marseille
1994	AC Milan
1995	Ajax
1996	
1997	

World Cup

1958	Brazil
1962	Brazil
1966	England
1970	Brazil
1974	West Germany
1978	Argentina
1982	Italy
1986	Argentina
1990	West Germany
1994	Brazil
1998	

European Cup Winners' Cup

1985	Everton		1992	Werder Bremen
1986	Dynamo Kiev		1993	Parma
1987	Ajax		1994	Arsenal
1988	Mechelen		1995	Real Zaragoza
1989	Barcelona		1996	
1990	Sampdoria		1997	
1991	Manchester United			

WE WAS ROBBED

CONTENTS

WE WOZ...

Football Facts

More Worms at Wembley

'Watch out!' cried the first worm
as the centre tried to shoot.
'You only just missed me
with your great big boot.'

'Yes, careful,' said the second,
'With your clumsy great hoof.
Just remember: you're running
about on our roof.'

Then the ball hit the net
and the crowd roared, 'GOAL!'
So the third worm simply sighed
and retreated down its hole.

Tony Mitton

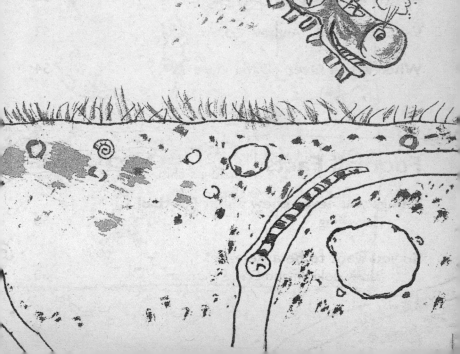

A Football Amulet

From the fans' throats
    the raucous roar,
The raucous roar
    then the goalkeeper's throw,

The goalkeeper's throw
    then the sweeper's pass,
The sweeper's pass
    then the full back's flick,

The full back's flick
    then the midfielder's chip,
The midfielder's chip
    then the winger's run,

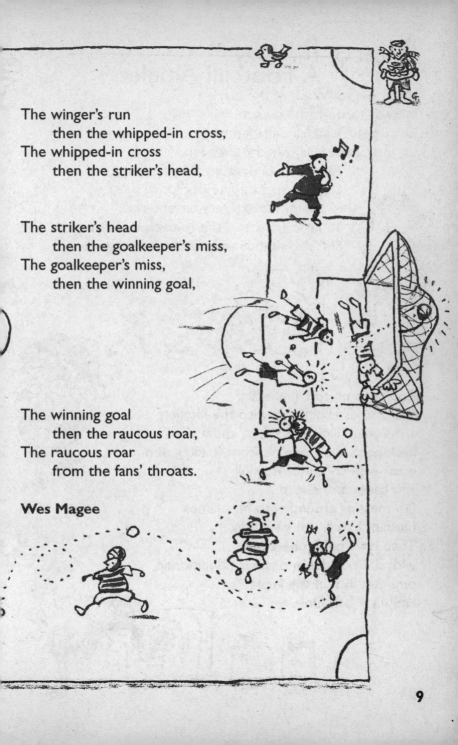

The winger's run
    then the whipped-in cross,
The whipped-in cross
    then the striker's head,

The striker's head
    then the goalkeeper's miss,
The goalkeeper's miss,
    then the winning goal,

The winning goal
    then the raucous roar,
The raucous roar
    from the fans' throats.

Wes Magee

Wash of the Day

Welcome to 'Wash of the Day',
midway through the season.
Once again it's Mrs Edna James
vs. the Castle Hill Primary team kit.
Always an interesting fixture this
and we've got a fine day for it.
Mrs James looks very determined.
So far this season she remains undefeated
and she intends to maintain her record.

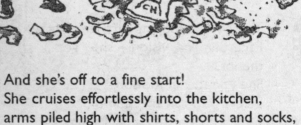

And she's off to a fine start!
She cruises effortlessly into the kitchen,
arms piled high with shirts, shorts and socks,
back-heels the washer's front-loading door
open with consummate skill
and bangs in the load.
No messing around with Mrs James.
No fancy stuff, just gets it in.
Then it's a quick one-two
with the powder and fabric conditioner,
one deft flick of the wrist
and it's Wash On!

The action's non-stop.
The kit soaks up the punishment.
But it's no contest.
Wash.
Rinse.
Spin dry
and then a quick transfer
to a laundry basket
and it's out into the back garden.

There's no stopping Mrs James now!
Pace, stamina, vision – she's got
the lot.
She's poetry in motion.
Before you can say 'non-bio'
she's got everything pegged-up.
What a line-up!
And it's all as clean as a whistle.
It's all over bar the shouting.
A sparkling performance!

What can you say about this woman?
She's sensational.
In a league of her own.

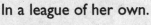

(To the tune of 'You'll Never Walk Alone':)

'Waaassh on! Waaassh on!
With soap from the start –
And you'll never wa-ash alone
You'll never waaassh a-lone!'

Tony Langham

12

Every Game's a Home Game with my Footy Family

Grandad's in the goal
Dad's in defence
Mother's in midfield
Baby's on the bench

Sister's centre forward
Brother's at the back
Cousin is the coach
Auntie's in attack

Nana is the manager
and just because I missed
a penalty last home match
I'm on the transfer list.

Paul Cookson

Penalty I

Which side shall I put it?
Which way will he go?
Will I look a total schnook,
Or will I be a hero?

Shall I try to place it
To his left or to his right?
Or shall I try to blast it high
With all my blinkin' might?

Perhaps he'll stand up straight to it,
I can never seem to tell.
I wish I knew what he's going to do,
I don't feel very well.

I suppose I'd better take it,
I'm drowning in my sweat;
Here I go, I'll keep it low,
IT'S IN THE BACK OF THE NET!!

Penalty II

Which side will he put it?
Which way will he go?
Will I look a total schnook,
Or will I be a hero?

Will he try to place it
To my left or to my right?
Or will he try to blast it high
With all his blinkin' might?

Perhaps I should stand up to it,
I can never seem to tell.
I wish I knew what he's going to do,
I don't feel very well.

Here he comes to take it,
I'm drowning in my sweat;
Here I go, I'll just . . . Oh no!
IT'S IN THE BACK OF THE NET!!

Mike Jubb

Oath Sworn by all New Footballs

Before each match I must take a deep breath
and hold it through the game.

I must at all times be round and resilient;
able to bounce back when floored.

I must accept the odd punch
with no thoughts of revenge.

I must put up with a good kicking
without thought of retaliation.

When trapped I must be patient until released.
When cornered the player determines my escape.
At throw-ins I must be
entirely in his hands.

Though often crossed I must not be cross.

For free kicks, penalties and dead balls
I must always know my place.

I must remain modest; though I cross the line
credit goes to the striker.

While on nodding acquaintance with the players
I must at all times remain impartial.

John C. Desmond

Gabby the Groundsman

His name's Mr Gabriel, but we call him Gabby,
He wears old wellies and his tracksuit's baggy,
He rolls his own fags and makes his own wine
– And Gabby brings the oranges on at half-time.

Gabby is the groundsman down at the Rec,
He wears an old scarf round his old, skinny neck,
He puts out the corner flags and paints in the lines
– And Gabby brings the oranges on at half-time.

If ever there's a problem, he's quite prepared to ref,
(You can call him anything you like, 'cos Gabby's stone deaf)
If ever there's a problem, he'll always run the line
– And Gabby brings the oranges on at half-time.

And if you ever lose a stud, Gabby's got a spare,
He once produced a set of shirts from God knows where;
We once forgot the ball and he said, *'Ee y'are, borrow mine!'*
– And Gabby brings the oranges on at half-time.

Lots of people laugh at him, they say he's just a joke
But everyone in our team thinks he's a great bloke,
He's like an extra player, he's the joker in the pack,
He ought to have a tracksuit with his name across the back,
He's always there supporting us, rain or shine
– And Gabby brings the oranges on at half-time.

We heard it as a rumour first; we thought, *It can't be true!*
But then the rumour spread around till everybody knew
And we were really proud of him, between me and you:
We heard it in the playground, we heard it in assembly,
We saw it on the telly and it made us go all trembly:

There was Gabby bringing the oranges
on at half-time at Wembley!

Tony Charles

Dazzling Derek

That's my dad shouting at me
from the touchline
like he does every game we play.

I don't know why
I think we do quite well really
this week we're only losing ten-one
and I've scored three times
twice in my goal
and once in theirs

not bad for a goalie.

Last week I was on the wing
it was brilliant
I nearly scored a million times
we still lost
but who was counting?

My dad was
he got really angry
there's no pleasing him.

What he really wants to do
is to shrink back to being ten like me
slip onto the field
score the winning goal
with seconds to go
defeat staring us in the face
Dazzling Derek saves the day!

But he can't
so he jumps up and down on the touchline
shouts at me
mutters and kicks the grass
stubs his toe and yells
nearly gets sent off the field by the ref

where's the fun in that?

David Harmer

"In your dreams, Derek"

Song of a Frustrated Scouse Winger

Over 'ere with it, Charlie!
Does it 'ave ter take a year!
On me 'ed, son, on me 'ed then,
let's 'ave it over 'ere!

Their back line's 'opeless,
goalie's a gormless clot.
Knock it over quick t' ruz,
I'll purrit in the pot!

Cum 'ed, Charlie, pass it, lad!
Are y gunna take all year?
To me left, me left foot, Charlie!
Curl it over 'ere!

D'y-raffter 'og it all yerself,
fumble it down the right,
when I am stalkin' on the left,
one big goal in sight?

A gapin' goal just dead ahead,
me properly onside
and you greedy-guts-in' with the ball,
bangin' it yards wide!

Matt Simpson

Making a Meal of It

What did you do at school today?

Played football.

Where are you going now?

To play football.

What time will you be back?

After football.

Football! Football! Football!
That's all I ever hear.

Well!

Well don't be late for tea.

OK.

We're having football casserole.

Eh?

Followed by football crumble.

What?

Washed down with a . . .

As if I can't guess!

nice pot of . . .

I'm not listening!

... tea.

Bernard Young

Football through the Ages

Football grew from itchy feet
kicking whatever they found in the street;
a pebble; a stick; a rolling stone;
a rusty can or an animal's bone.
The left-over bladder of a butchered pig,
inflated and tied off, was perfect to kick;
if something would roll it would do for the game
that then had not even been given a name
till, on through the ages, the game was to grow,
at long last becoming the football we know.

O, I'm glad of my football, I'm glad of the rules,
I'm glad of the pitches at clubs and at schools,
I'm glad of my kit, but I am even gladder
the days are long gone when they kicked a pig's bladder.

Celia Warren

Oddball

Who was it went and shifted
both sets of goalposts?
You can't see either net.
The pitch is so vast
there's no end to it, yet

the thick and nasty fog's not lifted,
there isn't a single sound.
You call and call for the ball
that's never seen or passed . . .

What's gone wrong, where are the teams?
You get an urge to take off, fast,
but with boots glued to the ground,
discover you can't move at all.

Whose are those screams?
You yell for the ref,
though the ref must be deaf:
he looks weirdly thin in that long black coat,
and then he whistles a very strange note

like nothing else you've ever heard,
before he floats off out of view.
You tell yourself you'd have preferred
staying at home – it's too cold here for you.

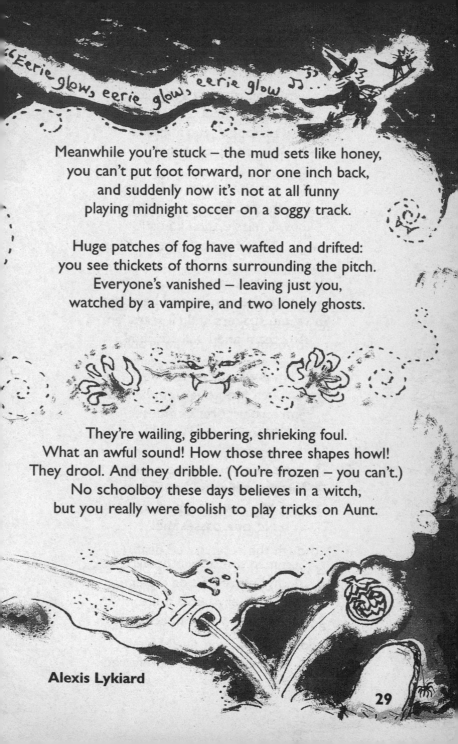

"Eerie glow, eerie glow, eerie glow ♫"...

Meanwhile you're stuck — the mud sets like honey,
you can't put foot forward, nor one inch back,
and suddenly now it's not at all funny
playing midnight soccer on a soggy track.

Huge patches of fog have wafted and drifted:
you see thickets of thorns surrounding the pitch.
Everyone's vanished — leaving just you,
watched by a vampire, and two lonely ghosts.

They're wailing, gibbering, shrieking foul.
What an awful sound! How those three shapes howl!
They drool. And they dribble. (You're frozen — you can't.)
No schoolboy these days believes in a witch,
but you really were foolish to play tricks on Aunt.

Alexis Lykiard

No One Passes Me

I'm a blaster not a tapper
I'm a ninety minute scrapper
I'm a chopper and a hacker
No one passes me!

I have got the brawn and muscle
For the tackle and the tussle
I will hassle and I'll hustle
No one passes me!

Harum-scarum do or dare 'em
I will take the knocks and bear 'em
Show me strikers and I'll scare 'em
Any team and I will stir 'em!

I'm a winner not a loser
I'm a rough 'em tough 'em bruiser
I'm a goalscorer's confuser
No one passes me!

I'm the one you love to send on
The defender you depend on
Strong of sinew, tough of tendon
No one passes me!

Summer sun or winter mire
Lion-hearted do or die-er
In my belly burns a fire
I'm the one who can inspire!

I'm a last ditch tackle fighter
I'm a knee and ankle biter
Nobody will mark you tighter
No one
No one
No one
No one
No one passes me!
Right!

Paul Cookson

Hate the Rain

Hate the rain
Said the boy
With the mud
In his eye
Soggy boots
Chilly legs
Boggy pants.

Give me rain
In my hair
Said the boy
In the chair.
Give me mud
On my boots
And my face.

Hate the rain
Said the boy
As his shot
Skidded wide
To the laughs
And the shouts
And the chants.

Give me
One chance to play
Just five seconds
Someday
Just one kick
Just one touch
In your place.

David Clayton

Playground Song

Footy in the playground
Red sun in the sky
I might play for England
Piggywigs might fly.

Johnny Mars picks Spanner
Johnny Mars picks Rose
Andy Platt picks Henry
Henry picks his nose.

Fifty running girls and boys
Screaming for the ball
One goal is the iron gates
One the lavvy wall.

Uuurgh! ...
You're
grim,
Henry!

Ghosts sit in our classroom
Ghosts climb up the stairs
Rows of ghostly children
Upright in our chairs.

Ghosts upon the school wall
Watching us each day
Crowding through the doorway
At the end of play.

Gareth Owen

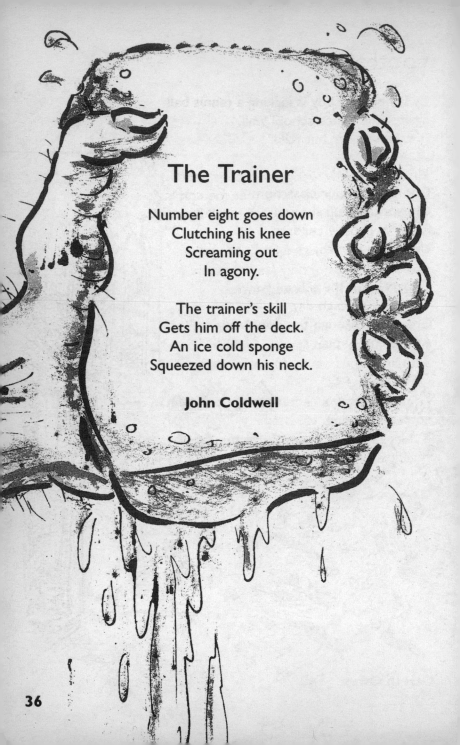

The Trainer

Number eight goes down
Clutching his knee
Screaming out
In agony.

The trainer's skill
Gets him off the deck.
An ice cold sponge
Squeezed down his neck.

John Coldwell

Footballer

By lamplight a boy is kicking a tennis ball
against the dance-school wall.
It is November but mild.

His hat is tightly wedged onto his head
and he hesitates when he sees me coming.
The street is quiet but for the ball drumming.

He makes an ungraceful angular shape
like most boys do, only his loneliness
smooths out his crooked angles.

It is as if someone long dead
had come back to life as a child
with ambitions he could not explain.

Something is wedged inside the bobble hat,
something wants to escape.
Running headlong out of dreams, the flat
realities hover about him like angels.

George Szirtes

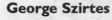

Football Report

The Bees gave the Magpies the bird,
    And the Cherries were ripe for the picking.
The Wolves and the Lions were both on the prowl
    And the Wanderers wandered round kicking.

The Gunners were playing some big shots,
    The Blues were all down in the dumps,
The Saints were no match for the Rangers,
    But the Stamford Bridge lot came up trumps.

The Spurs gave the Hammers a battering,
    The Robins played on in the snow,
The Hornets were buzzing and stinging,
    And the Rovers knew just where to go.

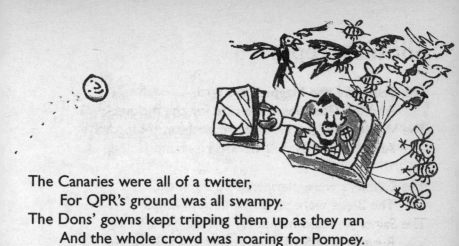

The Canaries were all of a twitter,
    For QPR's ground was all swampy.
The Dons' gowns kept tripping them up as they ran
    And the whole crowd was roaring for Pompey.

* * * * * * * * * * *

I hope you've enjoyed this short ditty!
    Can't think of much else to report,
So I'm off to the other Canaries –
    I've earned a suspension from sport!

Pam Gidney

RIP Offs

Here lies the body
Of your United,
Promotion hopes
Quite sadly blighted.
Meanwhile, my City's
Sitting pretty.

Here lies the body
Of your poor City.
Bribed our goalie!
What a pity!
City,
Shame of all the nation,
Doomed to three years'
Relegation!

Here lies the body
Of our centre back;
Beat his own goalie
With a wicked pass-back.

Here lies the body
Of a fool in the crowd:
Shouted rude words
Far too loud.

Here lies the body
Of a poor sad fan,
Faced with a life-long
Away-game ban.

Here lies the body
Of a player from City.
Got a free transfer.
What a pity!

Here lies the body
Of our first team coach,
More useless
Than an old cockroach.

Here lies the body
Of a hopeless winger.
Would have done better
As an opera singer.

Here lies the body
Of Brian Bowler,
Flattened to death
By the groundsman's roller.

Here lies the body
Of Bertie Bissell,
Swallowed the pea
In his referee's whistle.

John Kitching

41

Village Football Match, 1946

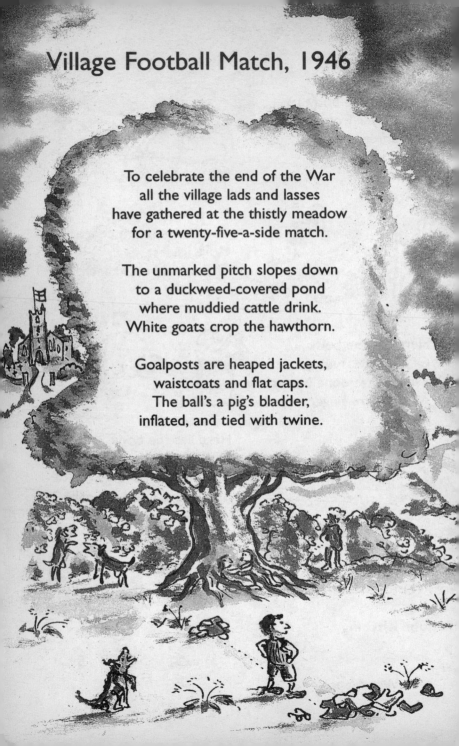

To celebrate the end of the War
all the village lads and lasses
have gathered at the thistly meadow
for a twenty-five-a-side match.

The unmarked pitch slopes down
to a duckweed-covered pond
where muddied cattle drink.
White goats crop the hawthorn.

Goalposts are heaped jackets,
waistcoats and flat caps.
The ball's a pig's bladder,
inflated, and tied with twine.

Endless, the game thunders on,
on into the gloaming.
It is nineteen-all
as the purple dusk deepens.

Now only three spectators remain:
an invalid-faced full moon,
a howling mongrel
and a single astonished star.

Wes Magee

Match of the Year

I am delivered to the stadium by chauffeur-driven
  limousine.
Gran and Grandpa give me a lift in their Mini.

I change into my sparkling clean world-famous designer
  strip.
*I put on my brother's shorts and the T-shirt with tomato
  ketchup stains.*

I give my lightweight professional boots a final shine.
I rub the mud off my trainers.

The coach gives me a final word of encouragement.
Dave, the sports master, tells me to get a move on.

I jog calmly through the tunnel out into the stadium.
I walk nervously onto the windy sports field.

The crowd roars.
Gran and Grandpa shout 'There's our Jimmy!'

The captain talks last minute tactics.
'Pass to me or I'll belt you.'

The whistle goes. The well oiled machine goes into
  action.
Where did the ball go?

I pass it skilfully to our international star, Bernicci.
*I kick it away. Luckily, Big Bernard stops it before it
  goes over the line.*

A free kick is awarded to the visiting Premier team. I'm
  part of the impregnable defence.
*The bloke taking the kick looks six feet tall – and just
  as wide . . .*

I stop the ball with a well-timed leap and head it
  expertly up the field.
The ball thwacks me on the head.

The crowd shouts my name! 'Jim-meee! Jim-meee!
  Jim-meee!'
Gran says, 'Eee, our Jim's fallen over.'

I don't remember any more.

Trevor Millum

Goal

There's kissing, there's shouting,
there's hugging and leaping
and swaying and singing
and a cheer from the whole
clan of supporters;
there are flags, there are banners,
there is huge celebration,
because Kenny, our hero, has scored a great goal.

O the pitch it is green with the greenness of summer,
and the roses exult, and the neighbours look over
the fence (is the cat being chased? no, thank goodness)
it is only young Kenny kicking a football
and shouting in triumph and letting the whole
neighbourhood know that he alone, Kenny,
in the back garden, sole king of the stadium,
Kenny the hero has scored a great goal.

Gerda Mayer

46

Never Put Noel in Goal

Damn! There goes another goal.
That must make it ten they stole.

Why do we suffer this terrible toll?
Because some prat put Noel in goal.

Oh, no! Not Noel.
He flaps around like a Dover sole.
We always get this rigmarole
whenever we've got Noel in goal.

So who gave Noel that role?
Who put Noel in goal?
I bet they think they're droll.

Give 'em jail with no parole.
They must be round the pole.

Noel, Noel, pathetic prole,
without one virtue to extol,
a sorry soul with no control.

Take a stroll, Noel.
Crawl back in your hole.
Quit the team, claim the dole.

A slightless mole'd
patrol our goal
better on the whole than you, Noel.

A frightened foal
could fill your role,
or a water vole
or a lump of coal.

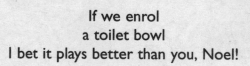

If we enrol
a toilet bowl
I bet it plays better than you, Noel!

Nick Toczek

Pantomime

HE'S BEHIND YER

shriek the red-faced fans behind the home goal.

HE'S BEHIND YER

as their red-haired keeper balances the ball on the
palm of one hand.

HE'S BEHIND YER

as the red-shirted away winger jabs the ball using his
head.

HE'S BEHIND YER too late as the red-raged keeper
screams,

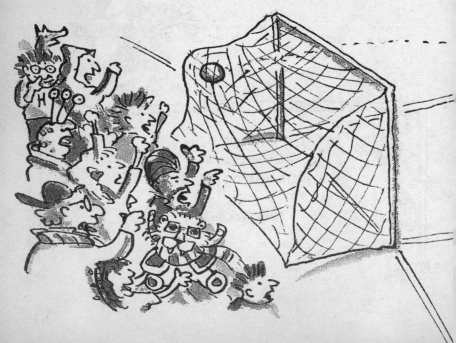

HE CAN'T DO THAT REF

OH YES HE CAN as the red-rippled net welcomes the
 ball.

OH NO HE CAN'T

OH YES HE CAN

OH NO HE CAN'T continues the red-carded keeper
 alone in the dressing room.

Ian Blackman

After the Match

Did yer see the other team?
Thee all 'ad one leg,
'ands tied behind their backs.
Ah've seen better schoolboys round our way
Kicking ball in't street.
Their kits were rubbish
Thee didn't even look the part,
More like rag and bone men.
Feller who trained 'em should ha'
Taught 'em to play football
Not nancy around with the ball
Like ballet dancers.
An' another thing.
That ref was blind
Or thee'd never ha' won.

Angela Topping

What a Team!

It's not their fancy footwork
it's not their certain skill,
it's not the way they kick the ball
that gives us such a thrill.

It's not their famous players
it's not the way they score;
it's our team's new outside loo
which makes the crowd all roar.

It's the football on the seat
to help pass the time of day,
it's the little potty underneath
for when they play away.

It's the way the toilet flushes
when someone scores a goal,
it's the name of every player
on every toilet roll.

It's the whistle on the wall
to blow when you're inside,
it's our team's new toilet
that makes their winning side.

Andrew Collett

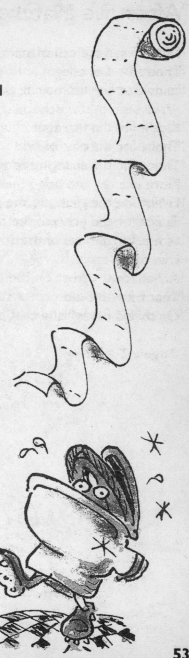

53

When it's all Over

It's not for the smell of stale embrocation,
It's not for the days of anticipation,
It's not for the fist-waving glad celebration;

It's not for the fear that churns up your gut,
It's not for the pair of odd socks for good luck,
It's not for the changing room door banging shut;

It's not for the glint and the gleam of the studs,
It's not for the echo of the ball's ringing thud,
It's not for the feel of the soft clinging mud;

It's not for the frost on the pitch in the morning,
It's not for the substitutes standing round yawning,
It's not for the whistle that blasts without warning;

It's not for the mist that swirls round the posts,
It's not for the other team shrouded like ghosts,
It's not for the spectators lost in their coats;

It's not for the sweat on your head when you're running,
It's not for the threat of legs bruised, grey and numbing,
It's not for the net that deceives you with cunning:

But when it's all over,
When it's all done,
Whether we've lost,
But best if we've won –
We break out the soap,
High spirits and towels,
And sing in the showers
For hours and hours.

Dave Ward

Football
Facts

Things you never knew about Football

Why are there always huge, grey, furry caterpillars clinging onto television cameras?

Why does the referee make the two captains stand in the middle of the pitch in pouring rain to toss the coin when they could have done that in the nice, warm changing rooms?

Why do referees look at least eighty years old?

Why do they make the bar just that little bit too high for the goalie to reach?

Why don't the captains ever let their mascots ever play for their teams and why do they run off with the triangular pendants they swap?

Why don't they let managers sit in proper seats instead of having to hide in a trench beside the pitch?

How do substitutes always manage to get their tracksuits off without snagging their studs on the material?

Why do goalkeepers spend the entire match shouting when nobody takes a blind bit of notice?

Why do you never notice the penalty spot until there's a penalty?

Why is it that the spectators of the losing team have to leave early?

Why do all defenders have short back and sides and super-star strikers have long, curly hair?

What does the goalie need a little bag for?

If linesmen need white sticks why doesn't the FA provide them?

Gary King

So you want to be a Referee?

**1. You forget your whistle at an important match.
Do you:**

a) cough politely each time there's a foul?

b) ask the players to own up when they commit an offence?

c) award penalties every two minutes until somebody wins?

**2. A player belches and doesn't say 'Pardon'.
Do you:**

a) give him an indigestion sweet?

b) give him a lecture and a yellow card for being so rude?

c) make him say 'Pardon me, Referee' really loudly over
the tannoy system?

**3. A player coughs, spits but leaves dribble down his face.
Do you:**

a) give him a tissue?

b) tell him to find a tissue?

c) hand the trainer a tissue?

**4. You catch the goalie making mud pies in the penalty
area. Do you:**

a) kick them over and flatten the pitch
as best you can?

b) give him a proper bucket and spade?

c) agree they are an acceptable line
of defence?

5. Two opposing players become involved in a physical tussle leading to punches being thrown. Do you:

a) pretend it hasn't happened until both sides have said sorry?

b) break it up and use your red card on them?

c) stand back and watch, give them a sharp kick in the shin when they aren't looking, then send them off?

6. A player disagrees with your decision and calls you a very rude name. Do you:

a) ask him to spell it while you write it down?

b) make him write 'I'm very sorry' 100 times?

c) call it him back with bells on?

7. It is a game at a neutral ground. Both teams play in blue and want to this time as well. Do you:

a) let them both play in blue and call it a draw?

b) toss a coin to see who changes shirts?

c) make both teams take their shirts off and paint their chests a different colour?

8. A player falls harmlessly to the ground then writhes around clutching his leg. Do you:

a) get the opposition to help him up and rub his knee better?

b) stop the game and bring on the trainer with the stretcher even though everyone knows in three minutes he'll be leaping around like a gazelle in football boots?

c) kick his other leg and send him off for time-wasting?

9. A delicate situation happens in front of you but you miss it because you're daydreaming.
Do you:

a) ask the players to re-enact the situation in slow motion so that you can make the correct decision?

b) pretend there's dirt in your eye and get the linesman to sort it out?

c) ignore it and carry on the game, sending off anyone who argues?

10. It is the last five minutes of a Cup Final. The scores are level. You are hungry and want your tea. There is a dubious appeal for a penalty.
Do you:

a) ignore it, uphold fair play and stay hungry?

b) go and get a pie from the pie-seller and then ignore the appeal?

c) give the penalty, finish the game early, and nip out for a double fish and chips and a greasy burger?

11. Halfway through the first half a young player lets you know that he needs the toilet.
   Do you:
a) let him go back to the changing rooms?
b) tell him he should have thought of that before you started but OK, go anyway?
c) get the trainer to run on with a bucket?

12. One captain says his team have all got colds and can they wear their woolly jumpers, scarves and tracky bottoms.
   Do you:
a) say yes as long as they don't get too hot and faint?
b) check they all have a note from their mums?
c) say no and make them play in their pants and vests?

If you scored mainly:
a) You softy.
b) You wishy-washy wet blanket.
c) You nasty person, you'll grow up to be a
head teacher, or even a dinner lady!

Paul Cookson and David Harmer

TROPHIES

Extra Time Quiz

Look at the drawings on pages 56 to 63.
Can you find these people
in the poems earlier in the book?
Go to the top of the Premier League
if you can find all of them!

THEY THINK IT'S ALL OVER!

Contents

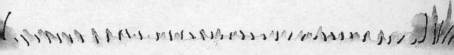

Kick-off

'Get ready,' says the worm
as the crowd begins to roar.
'Here comes the kick-off
for football book four.

'In between passes
look hard and you'll see
a wriggly little feller —
yup! That's me.'

Tony Mitton

Ten–Nil

The phantom fans are chanting
There's a cheer in my ear as I score:
I've done it again: ten goals to me
And nil to the garage door!

Celia Warren

Dick Tater

I am a little linesman.
I've got a little flag.
Oh, how I love to waggle it.
Wag, wag, wag, wag, wag, wag.

My happiest of memories
(I laughed until I cried!)
Was when that striker
Scored three times,
But I signalled him offside!

(It was curious
To see him so furious.)

John Kitching

Dream Team Song

They're the red vest on the robin
  they're the snowy mountain tops
they're an ocean liner bobbin'
  they're as fast as Keystone Kops
they're the currant in the bun
  and they're hotter
    yes, they're hotter
      yes, they're hotter
        than the sun!

They're the blossom on the cherry
   they're the gifts around the tree
they're the Frenchman's natty beret
   they're the surfer on the sea
they're a fairground filled with fun
   and they're hotter
      yes, they're hotter
         yes, they're hotter
            than the sun!

Wes Magee

Pitch Switch

When you meet me in the street
I'm clumsy on my feet
Is my footwork kinda neat?
No. It's not.

When you haul me back to school
I'm the sort that acts the fool
Thinks he's really cool
But he's not.

When you see me in the town
Pretending I'm a clown
The smartest guy around?
Am I? Not!

But when I'm on the pitch
It's like someone flicks a switch
When I get the ball
I'm all of six foot tall
And when I see the goal
I'm really on a roll
I'm a hero! I'm a giant!
I'm incredible! I'm defiant!
I'm a thousand million billion miles better than the rest!
For all of 90 minutes
I'm the BEST!

Trevor Millum

The World's Most Expensive Footballer

The world's most expensive footballer
has credit cards dripping from his fingertips,
his girlfriend tells of his gold-plated lips,
the studs on his boots have diamond tips.

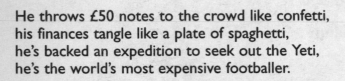

Pound coins fall from his trouser pocket,
under floodlights he glows like a rocket,
he's electrical with no need of a socket,
he's the world's most expensive footballer.

He throws £50 notes to the crowd like confetti,
his finances tangle like a plate of spaghetti,
he's backed an expedition to seek out the Yeti,
he's the world's most expensive footballer.

He dazzles spectators with his fancy passes,
don't stare at him without wearing sunglasses,
all other players his skill surpasses,
he's the world's most expensive footballer.

Brian Moses

Gran's XI

My grandma's in a football team.
Her age is seventy-eight.
She's no longer like a palm tree
Standing waiting for a date.

The goalie in my grandma's team,
Her age is seventy-four.
Opponents rarely score a goal.
She's built like a grey barn door.

The striker is a real antique,
Captain at eighty-eight.
She's vicious, mean, and fouls a lot;
The kind of striker goalies hate.

Two of Grandma's football team
Are quite acutely deaf.
They shout and wave most rudely
At every weekend ref.

When the red, red robin
Goes 606, bob, bobbing along

Most of Grandma's football team
Have aged, aching bones,
But in the showers, after games,
No single player moans.

The other week – a rare defeat.
They lost: three goals to five.
But they don't seem to care a lot.
They're just glad to be alive!

John Kitching

Referee, There's a Dog on the Pitch!

'Referee, Referee,
There's a dog on the pitch,'
The player said.

'Referee, Referee,
The dog's dribbling the ball,'
The player cried.

'Referee, Referee,
The dog's won a tackle,'
The player shouted.

'Referee, Referee,
The dog's just been fouled,'
The player yelled.

'Referee, Referee,
The dog's taken a free kick,'
The player screamed.

'Referee, Referee,
The dog's just scored,'
The player growled.

The referee sighed.
He pulled out a red card
And sent the player off.

The team manager substituted another player,
Spot the dog ran onto the pitch
To a tumultuous reception from the crowd
And went on to score the winning goal.

Margaret Blount

The Manager's Lament

'We'll get a result,' the manager said,
'Cos we're comfortable on the ball.
'Pace at the front and sound at the back,
And we make no mistakes at all.'

'We've vision and skill,' the manager said,
'And we play with a flat back four.
Midfield is strong and Jonesy's in form
And our Robbo knows how to score.'

'We'd no luck at all,' the manager said,
When the team had gone down six–two.
'Two goals offside and one was a foul,
And the ref? He hadn't a clue.'

Redvers Brandling

Rainbow Mad

I don't mind
when my ears go red,
when everyone stares
at something I've said.

I don't care
when my fingers turn blue,
when I've missed the bus
and I'm freezing through.

I'm not bothered
when my face looks green,
when I've read horror stories
and think I've seen

vampires and monsters
with slimy purple eyes,
yellow fang-like teeth
five times the normal size.

But I hate it, can't take it,
turn every colour there's ever been,
when I play for our team —
aim at goal . . . and miss.

Joan Poulson

The Start of my Career

I've been picked?
I've really been picked?
You mean I've been picked for the football team?

Pinch me hard.
Wake me up.
Can this be a dream?

No dream!

You've been picked.
You've really been picked.
You have been picked for the football team.

You're the substitute's substitute's substitute
so you'll probably not
get a game.

But we need to know you're ready.
Able. Willing. Keen.
The second eleven might need you.
Come running if we call your name.

Because you've been picked.
You've really been picked.
You have been picked for the football team.

Wow!

Team

James S.
Tinribs
Gopinda
Kaiya
Amy
Olivia
Gaby M.
Thomas
Marianne M.
Anil B.
Andrew
Sub.
Tabitha
Sub. Sub.
Jonesy
Sub. Sub. Sub.
Simon S.

Iron my kit.
Polish my boots.
I'm the substitute's substitute's substitute.

The substitute's substitute's substitute:
I'll probably not
get a game.

The substitute's substitute's substitute:
I'm honoured
all the same.

I'm usually ignored.

But now
    I've been picked

I've sort of
    been picked

I've almost
    been picked

For the Football Team.

(It's a start.)

Bernard Young

Football Strip

They call me Bottomless Barrymore Blue,
I'm famous around the town
for everyone knows, when I kick a ball,
my trousers come tumbling down.

I've tried some old braces knotted with string
but it's the same if ever I score;
I feel a low rumble deep down below
as my trousers slip to the floor.

So I've an idea to help football players
whose trousers don't seem to fit:
just wear a long jumper down to your knees
instead of your old football kit.

Andrew Collett

oops!

Exit

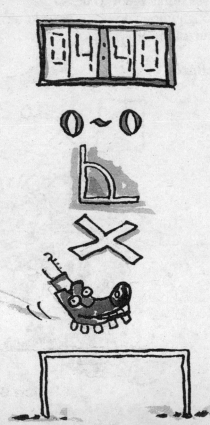

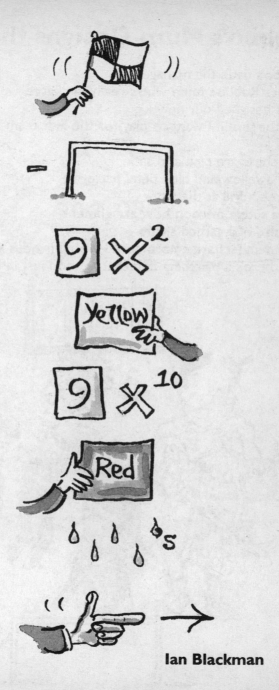

Ian Blackman

Robbo's Mum Designs the Kit

Robbo's dad's the manager
but it's Robbo's mum who's really in charge.
She's designed our new kit . . .
I'm not sure if I want to play for the first team any more.

The shirts are pink and satin
with a yellow and blue petal pattern
There's a frill at the front
and a subtle maroon bow attachment
the size of a garden shrub.
Our numbers are embroidered with luminous sequins
and there's a matching detachable hood just in case it rains.

The shorts are available in a range of corresponding colours:
lemon, lime or raspberry
and the stockings are Lycra
with gold and silver thread
and held up with silk garters that have a rosette motif.

At least there's one thing . . .
we never clash kits with other teams.

Mind you, the platform football boots
were a bit too much.
Even Robbo's dad said we didn't have to wear them
as he adjusted his gold lamé puff-sleeved tracksuit.

Paul Cookson

Desperate for Help

He'd let in 87 goals
With the season still yet young,
And all the fans made fun of him –
His goalie's pride was stung.

So imagine how he must have felt
When a stranger said one day,
'I'll help you, son, I'll soon improve
The standard of your play.'

'Wow,' he said, 'that's great, that's great.
It'll help restore my pride.
Are you a goalkeeper yourself?'
'No – an optician,' he replied . . .

Clive Webster

This Lad's No Fool

He'd applied for a trial with a top football club,
And they'd said, 'Come tomorrow at one.'
He arrived with his kit, all eager and keen,
But alas, the poor lad's brain had gone.

The manager said, 'Can you kick with both feet?'
The lad gave a grin and replied,
'If I kicked with both feet I'd fall flat on my bum,
I'm not stupid.' The manager cried . . .

Clive Webster

My Mum's put me on the Transfer List

On Offer:
one nippy striker, ten years old
has scored seven goals this season
has nifty footwork and a big smile
knows how to dive in the penalty box
can get filthy and muddy within two minutes
guaranteed to wreck his kit each week
this is a FREE TRANSFER
but he comes with running expenses
weeks of washing shirts and shorts
socks and vests, a pair of trainers
needs to scoff huge amounts
of chips and burgers, beans and apples
pop and cola, crisps and oranges
endless packets of chewing gum.
This offer open until the end of the season
I'll have him back then
at least until the cricket starts.
Any takers?

David Harmer

Harry Commentator Says . . .

It's the one we've been waiting for,
It's a game of two halves,
A classic all the way through,
Yet another unique match,
Between two of the best,
With everything to do,
Being put to the test,
At this present moment in time,
With a mountain to climb,
They'll try to close them down in the open,
And open them up at the back,
Keeping it tight in midfield,
And working out some slack,
Looking for a quick goal,
To rock their opponents,
And knock them for six.
At the end of the day,
It's goals that count,
They've got it all to do!
Today,
And every day like it,
And I have to say,
That this unforgettable clash
Between . . . er . . . er . . . er . . . um!

Ian Larmont

New Kit

We were shocked by the colour of our new kit
Which looked like a dog had been sick on it.
It had shirt collars wider
Than the wings of a glider.
The shorts were ankle length – with braces,
The high-heel boots had zips, not laces.

So we made our protest on the football pitch
And played our first game without a stitch.

John Coldwell

Foregone Conclusion

The poor old football manager
Just didn't know what to do –
His team were bottom of the league,
They hadn't got a clue.

He thought, 'Some extra practice
Will do the beggars good.
We'll have a go this Sunday' –
The poor misguided pud.

He got eleven dustbins
And put them all in place,
The normal set-up, 4-4-2,
A smug look on his face.

'Right, lads, all you have to do
Is dribble round each bin,
Push the ball in front of you
And then just shoot it in.'

Alas, the session didn't work,
Despite the extra drill,
The dustbins played his team to death —
And won eleven–nil . . .

Clive Webster

Football Training

Monday
Practised heading the ball:
Missed it — nutted the neighbours' wall!

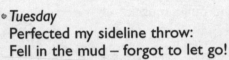

Tuesday
Perfected my sideline throw:
Fell in the mud — forgot to let go!

Wednesday
Worked on my penalty kick:
A real bruiser — my toe met a brick.

Thursday
Gained stamina — went for jog:
Ran round in circles — lost in the fog!

Friday
Developed my tactical play:
Tackled a goalpost — it got in the way.

Saturday
Exercised — twenty-eight press-ups:
Did pull a muscle — but no major mess-ups.

Sunday
At last — the day of the match,
Came through it all without a scratch.
The ref was amazed how I kept my nerve;
He agreed it's not easy to be the reserve!

Celia Warren

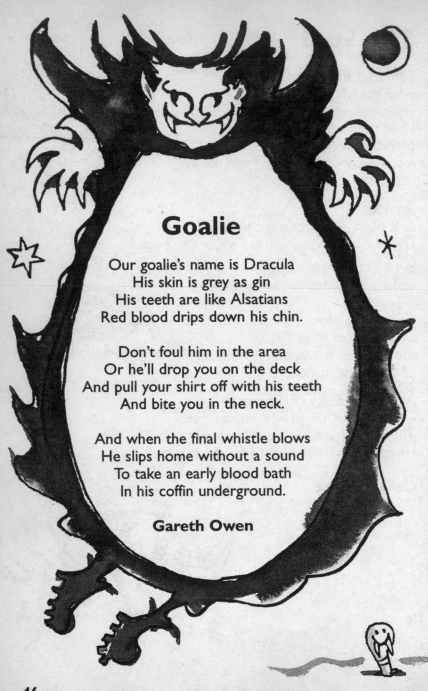

Goalie

Our goalie's name is Dracula
His skin is grey as gin
His teeth are like Alsatians
Red blood drips down his chin.

Don't foul him in the area
Or he'll drop you on the deck
And pull your shirt off with his teeth
And bite you in the neck.

And when the final whistle blows
He slips home without a sound
To take an early blood bath
In his coffin underground.

Gareth Owen

The Stud

I am the stud
who got left in the mud
while the others went home on the boot.
I had the bad luck
to get thoroughly stuck
just as everyone shouted out 'Shoot!'

Our goalscoring ace
fell down flat on his face
as he miskicked the ball and spun round.
He pulled at the sludge
but I just wouldn't budge
so he left me behind in the ground.

So now I'm alone.
Everyone has gone home,
and another stud's taking my place.
I'll stay here stuck fast
dreaming of glories past
till the grass grows and covers my face.

Brian K. Asbury

The Football Family Man

I'm the finest fan
that football's had.
I've a football gran
with a football fad.
I've a football mother
and a football dad.
And my football brother
has football bad.

With my football wife
in our football pad
to our football life
we football add
two football daughters
and a football lad,
all football supporters,
all football mad.

We've football dogs.
They're football clad
in football togs
like a football ad.
For our football ways,
we're football glad.
Without football days
we'd be football sad.

I'm a football man
who's football mad.
I'm the finest fan
that football's had.
I'm the football family man.

Nick Toczek

49

T' Flies v T' Fleas

The flies played the fleas on a saucer.
At half time they were three—nil up.
The flies' captain said, 'If nowt goes wrong
We'll be playing in t' final in t' cup.'

Ian Larmont

The Grandstand Grans

Eddie's gran and
Sammy's gran,
super-subbing Jammy's gran;

Bazza's gran and
Nicky's gran,
his Auntie Mel with Micky's gran.

They throng along, in hats and scarves,
to watch us every week.
Shouting out
'Away the lads!'
till each can hardly speak.

Robbo's gran and
Rafique's gran
with his cousin Sadiq's gran;

Stewpot's gran and
Andy's gran;
side by side – the Grandstand grans.

Flasks of tea and sandwiches
keep them warm, come rain or shine.
We rarely lose,
now they support –
and the loudest one is mine!

Mike Johnson

Last Word

Said the pitch
to the grandstand,
'I'm old and I'm lined;
Life seems so flat
After all these years.'

Said the grandstand
to the pitch,
'Well, never mind;
I'm so unhappy
My seats are in tiers.'

Trevor Millum

The Night I Won the Cup

Last night I had a wonderful dream,
Dreamed I was the captain of the England football team.
Running on the pitch, feeling ever so proud,
Hearing the roar of the capacity crowd

Shouting, cheering,
Booing, jeering,
Oohing and aahing,
As the game got underway.

It was nearly full-time. There was still no score.
It looked like we'd have to settle for a draw.
From deep in defence we developed an attack.
I jinked and I swerved. I was past their full-back.

And the crowd started shouting:

Whack it! Smack it!
Give it all you've got!
Swerve it! Curve it!
Go on! Take a shot!

The goalie rushed out to do the best he could.
I kept my head down as a striker should.
Into the net, the football soared.
The crowd went mad. Everyone roared.

It's a goal! It's a goal!
He's scored! He's scored!
They were hand-clapping, back-slapping,
Yelling, jumping up.
He's done it! We've done it!
We've won the cup!

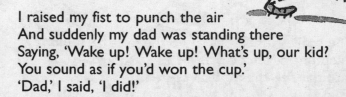

I raised my fist to punch the air
And suddenly my dad was standing there
Saying, 'Wake up! Wake up! What's up, our kid?
You sound as if you'd won the cup.'
'Dad,' I said, 'I did!'

John Foster

Final Whistle

The crowd went wild
as the final whistle blew.
But down in his hole
the worm breathed, 'Phew!

'The things they do up there
are quite beyond belief.
Thank goodness it's over.
What a relief!'

Tony Mitton

We Are Not Alone!

Paranormal poems chosen by Paul Cookson

Ready Salted

Nothing else happened
   that day.

Nothing much, anyway.

I got up, went to school,
   did the usual stuff.

Came home, watched telly,
   did the usual stuff.

Nothing else happened
   that day.

Nothing much, anyway,

but the eyeball in the crisps
   was enough.

            Ian McMillan

YOU'LL NEVER WALK ALONE

More football poems
chosen by David Orme

A Perfect Match

We met in Nottingham Forest,
    My sweet Airdrie and I.
She smiled and said, 'Alloa!' to me –
    Oh, never say goodbye!

I asked her, 'Is your Motherwell?'
    And she replied, 'I fear
She's got the Academicals
    From drinking too much beer.'

We sat down on a Meadowbank
    And of my love I spoke.
'Queen of the South,' I said to her,
    'My fires of love you Stoke!'

We went to Sheffield, Wednesday.
    Our Hearts were one. Said she:
'Let's wed in Accrington, Stanley,
    Then we'll United be.'

The ring was Stirling silver,
    Our friends, Forfar and wide,
A motley Crewe, all gathered there
    and fought to kiss the bride.

The best man had an awful lisp.
    'Come Raith your glatheth up,'
He said, and each man raised on high
    His Coca-Cola cup.

The honeymoon was spent abroad:
    We flew out east by Ayr,
And found the far-off Orient
    Partick-ularly fair.

We're home, in our own Villa now,
    (The Walsall painted grey)
And on our Chesterfield we sit
    And watch Match of the Day.

Pam Gidney

Nothing Tastes Quite Like a Gerbil
And other vile verses
chosen by David Orme

Nothing Tastes Quite Like a Gerbil

Nothing tastes quite like a gerbil
They're small and tasty to eat –
Morsels of sweet rodent protein
From whiskers to cute little feet!

You can bake them, roast them or fry them,
They grill nicely and you can have them en croute,
In garlic butter they're simply delicious
You can even serve them with fruit.

So you can keep your beef and your chicken,
Your lamb and your ham on the bone,
I'll have gerbil as my daily diet
And what's more – I can breed them at home!

Tony Langham

A selected list of poetry books available from Macmillan

The prices shown below are correct at the time of going to press. However, Macmillan Publishers reserve the right to show new retail prices on covers which may differ from those previously advertised.

The Secret Lives of Teachers	0 330 34265 7
Revealing rhymes, chosen by Brian Moses	£3.50
'Ere we Go!	0 330 32986 3
Football poems, chosen by David Orme	£2.99
You'll Never Walk Alone	0 330 33787 4
More football poems, chosen by David Orme	£2.99
Nothing Tastes Quite Like a Gerbil	0 330 34632 6
And other vile verses, chosen by David Orme	£2.99
Custard Pie	0 330 33992 3
Poems that are jokes, chosen by Pie Corbett	£2.99
nt-Free Zone	0 330 34554 0
Poems about parents, chosen by Brian Moses	£2.99
gue Twisters and Tonsil Twizzlers	0 330 34941 4
Poems chosen by Paul Cookson	£2.99

All Macmillan titles can be ordered at your local bookshop or are available by post from:

Book Service by Post
PO Box 29, Douglas, Isle of Man IM99 1BQ

Credit cards accepted. For details:
Telephone: 01624 675137
Fax: 01624 670923
E-mail: bookshop@enterprise.net

Free postage and packing in the UK.
Overseas customers: add £1 per book (paperback)
and £3 per book (hardback).

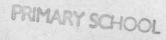